FIFTY MILLION FUTURES

A PROPOSAL FOR A RADICALLY NEW PUBLIC SCHOOL SYSTEM

TERENCE W. ROGERS PhD

FIFTY MILLION FUTURES

A PROPOSAL FOR A RADICALLY NEW PUBLIC SCHOOL SYSTEM

TERENCE W. ROGERS PhD

International Psychoanalytic Books (IPBooks)
New York • IPBooks.net

Copyright © 2019 Terence W. Rogers and IPBooks

International Psychoanalytic Books (IPBooks)
Queens, New York
Online at: www.IPBooks.net

All rights reserved. This book may not be reproduced, transmitted, or stored in whole or in part by any means, including graphic, electronic, or mechanical without the express permission of the publisher except in the case of brief quotations embodied in critical articles and reviews.

Cover design by Kathy Kovacic, Blackthorn Studio
Book design by Dan Williams
Back cover design by Dan Williams

ISBN: 978-1-949093-26-1

Printed in the United States of America

To my personal Futures,
Arianna, Christian and Sabina

ACKNOWLEDGEMENTS

Writing can be a lonely occupation, and requires the nourishment of a supportive environment. I have been blessed with many people willing to encourage and support this effort over a period of years.

My family has born the brunt of this effort and I owe them a deep debt of gratitude for their loving support. Without them this book would not have happened.

Among the many people who freely offered advice, questions and debate a few stand out for their willingness to continually engage without destroying the positive spirit that I hope is infused throughout this book. Robert Sibley has been a friend, co-creator, critic and source of much detailed information about the reality of schools, and Pat Sibley has kept us both on track when our ideas showed signs of running away with us.

Patricia Samara has been a constant source of energy to make it happen, and a constant reminder to think about the reader. She is passionate about the need to help children learn and find their own place in the world.

The final birth pangs have been greatly ameliorated by the professionalism and support of Tamara and Ahron at IPBooks. My grateful thanks go to them.

Finally I must thank the many people throughout the world who participated in the organizing of the International ThinkQuest Program during my time as its President and CEO. I learned from them just how far a small but dedicated group can go in changing the lives of teenagers, by treating them as independent people with ideas and the commitment to work and achieve. I learned from them that, by putting the students first and trusting their intentions, miracles can occur. This book is directly the result of what they taught was possible.

TABLE OF CONTENTS

Foreword IX

Chapter One: Overview 1
    The Forces Guiding Our Current System   3
    1. How Did Our Current System Arise?   3
    2. What organizes and Sustains Our Current School System?   4
    3. Which Educational Ideas Guide Daily School Activity?   5
    Another Key Element: Stability and Harmony   8
    Updating The Three Forces   9
    Updating The organizational Model: An Overview   10
    Updating Equal Opportunity: An Overview   11
    Updating Our Educational Ideas: An Overview   14
    Stability and The Three Modern Forces   16
    Designing A New School System: An Overview   17

Chapter 2: Equal Opportunity Revisited 21
    The New Social Compact For Learning   22
    The New Social Compact   22
    Natural Rights   23
    Students Rights and Parents Rights   25
    The Challenge of Taking Responsibility   26
    The Constitutional Issue   27
    In Brief   27
    The New Social Compact For Learning   28

Chapter 3: The School System Reorganized . . . 31
    The Elements of The *fmf* School System   32
    1. The Role of The State   33
    2. The *fmf* School System   34
    3. An Individual *fmf* School   36

    4. How Teachers Fit Into This Legal
        Structure.   38
    5. How Students Fit Into This Legal
        Structure   40
    6. Funding of *fmf* Schools   41
    Learning Centers and Counselors   42
    In Brief   44

Chapter 4: The Classroom Redefined 47
    The Educational Philosophy   47
    Standards   48
    Benefits To Teachers and Students   49
    Defining Standards For
        A Complex New World   50
    Standards and Equal Opportunity   50
    Standards, Careers and Motivating Students   52
    Standards Boards   53
    Public Confidence In Standards   54
    Dealing With Politically Contentious Issues   55
    The New 3R's Standards Board   55
    The New Civics Standards Board   56
    Defining Standards For The Liberal Arts
        Curriculum   58
    Standards For Employment   59
    Internal School Standards   60
    Certificates   60
    Assessment   61
    The Curriculum   63
    Many Paths To Success   63
    The *fmf* Curriculum and Society's Needs   64
    The New Mandatory Curriculum   65
    The New Elective Curriculum   66
    Learning How To Learn   67
    How People Learn   68
    The Facts or Critical Thinking   69
    Student, Know Thyself!   72

Practical Knowledge and Conceptual
    Knowledge   73
Why Are We Sitting In This Classroom?   75
Teachers and Classrooms   76
Types of School   79
In Brief   81

Chapter 5: Technology, The Great Enabler 85
Knowledge and Knowledge Technology   87
A Very Short History of Writing   88
Knowledge Technology, Version 2.   89
What Will It Mean To "Know"?   90
Version 2 Knowledge and fmf Schools   92
New Dangers   94
Technology or Textbooks   94
Looking Forward   97

Questions & Answers 101

Appendix 1 107
Today's Curriculum and Its Challenges   107
Predicting The Future   107
The Current 3R's Curriculum   108
The Current Vocational Curriculum   109
The Current Liberal Arts Curriculum   111

Appendix 2 115
Useful Data   115
Elementary and Secondary Education   115

Bibliography With Comments. 119
An Alternative View   130
Organizations and Schools Active In The
    Reform Movement (2018)   130

FOREWORD

The many books and papers written about our public school system are bitterly divided over what to do, but share one thing in common - they identify the problem as reforming our current system. They propose changing some specific part of the system as the key to transforming it. This book is entirely different. It proposes a completely new model of how a modern public school should be designed and function. It starts from the premise that the current system is beautifully designed to satisfy out of date objectives, and inherently resists changes, either by rejecting them or by rendering them ineffective.

The only way out of this dilemma is to design a new system, whose parts fit equally well together to meet new objectives in new ways. This book proposes such a new system, including the principles needed to guide it, and specific prescriptions for many of its aspects, including the roles of students, parents, teachers and the State; the key legal and financial controls, and the more typical topics such as the standards, the curriculum, the assessments and the classroom. Technology eventually plays a key role as an enabler, but features mostly in Chapter 5, where we discuss how knowledge is changing.

The challenge for the reader is to have a relevant context for assessing each part of the proposal as it flows in the natural linear order of a book. For example, the idea that students should decide when to take an important test makes little sense in the current system, but perfect sense in the new system, but the reader may not have covered the relevant parts of the description to make that judgment.

To overcome some of this difficulty, we suggest several possibilities. Use Chapter 1 to get an overview of the ideas, and then try to suspend judgment on individual parts of the proposal until the end. Chapters 2, 3 and 4 have an In Brief summary at the end, and readers may find it helpful to skip through some chapters to the summaries, if they are more interested in particular topics. We have tried to use lots of subheadings so that it is easier to go back to reread a topic.

Based on the reactions to verbal presentations of these ideas, the single commonest reaction is that such an enormous change is just too hard, both conceptually and practically. We Americans have not shown ourselves recently to be adept at addressing long term problems, and the public school system affects the majority of people in important ways. But we have made enormous social changes in the last thirty years, and we are at our best when fighting for high ideals. Surely, radically improving the ability of our children and grandchildren to survive, prosper and pursue happiness is one of the highest ideals we can fight for, and a prerequisite for engaging in that fight is to have a clear picture of the possibility we are fighting for.

The purpose of this book is to provide one such picture, and to stimulate others to add their vision at the same level of ambition as this proposal - a transformation that enables schools to perform and change with the best enterprises in the new global society.

If we, as a nation, are to remain a leader in the twenty first century, we must be a leader in the fights to manage the world's climate and to recruit new technologies to improve our lives without incurring unacceptable side effects. However, hidden among the prerequisites for managing those problems is our ability to educate our citizens to find the solutions and create a society that incorporates them. And buried at the root of that challenge is our desperate lack of knowledge as to how learners learn and how teachers can best teach.

At some point we will emulate in the field of Learning those efforts that we have created in Genetics, Space science, Nanoscience, Neuroscience and Information Technology. Namely we will have a focussed long term national effort to understand and to implement a sophisticated technology-backed approach to helping students to learn.

We hope this book provides a small contribution to energizing such an effort and the accompanying transformation of our public schools.

1.
OVERVIEW

We have reached the point where reforming our schools is not enough; we need to re-engineer them, re-evaluating their foundational ideas and social purpose, rebuilding them with modern techniques and organizational styles, removing the limitations of some of our most cherished educational ideas, and adopting radical new practices: in short, creating an institution capable of dealing with the new wave of problems threatening our well-being and our society.

These school problems belong with other fundamental problems of our industrial society: the dependence on rapidly disappearing cheap energy, the side effects on the environment of our prodigious use of energy, and the dependence on cheap labor, which transfers economic power to hungry Asian countries and leaves vast open spaces in the American economy – all problems causing enormous social and economic changes. When, inevitably, we turn to our schools for solutions to these problems, the inadequacy of our current schools will become even clearer.

Even measured against the "universal education" objectives of the twentieth century, our current schools are failing to deal with longstanding problems – such as the educational achievement gap between wealthy white suburban children and the mostly minority urban children - and exhibit a culture unable to enact large scale reform, preferring to look back to past successes and to argue about current failures rather than search for new opportunities.

Before shifting our focus to these opportunities, we should first acknowledge just how successful our schools were in tackling massive challenges: educating poor farm children and illiterate immigrants, binding many nationalities into one American nation, supplying the most effective industrial workforce in the world, and providing a path to higher education for millions of children who would otherwise have languished in poverty. These were the challenges and opportunities of two centuries ago, and, in accepting those challenges, our public schools have in large measure fulfilled one of the great aspirations of American society – equal opportunity through equal education.

Accepting this particular challenge was part of a great

unspoken bargain between educators and the public, cementing a bond between them that has lasted until very recently, a bond that generated resources and political support and contributed immeasurably to the stability of the school system in the face of significant upheavals. Re-energizing that bond must be one of the priorities of any attempt to re-engineer the school system, and energy will return when schools find a worthwhile successor to the "equal opportunity" role: a new role that once again uplifts us and provides us with hope for a better world for our children.

In searching for that new role, we can learn much from the program to re-engineer schools undertaken by nineteenth century educators and public leaders. They too faced enormous upheavals and daunting social challenges, while attempting to create for the first time in history a universally accessible public school system. Whether consciously or intuitively they found ways to overcome enormous practical and organizational challenges on the way to realizing their novel vision of schooling, one that fitted with their new social and industrial order. At the time it was a messy contentious struggle, but with the benefit of hindsight we can extract the key elements that led to its success and use them to create a new school system.

We can go further. We can reinterpret their basic approach in a modern context to provide a relatively detailed blueprint for a modern school system, and in doing so reap multiple advantages: past successes can be converted into future opportunities; the transition to the new system is more natural, and we eliminate many of the arbitrary or faddish reform ideas that do not scale.

Following this path, we come naturally to a prescription for selecting the characteristics of a desirable twenty-first century school system: first identify the historical major forces that have shaped our current school system, then understand the modern form of those forces, and finally examine whether and how these new forces naturally create a specific shape for the future system. The remainder of this chapter and several subsequent chapters follow through with this prescription and produce surprisingly concrete proposals for future schools, addressing, for example, how they should be organized and funded, how they should relate to students and parents, how standards should be set and students evaluated and much more.

This Overview provides a brief sketch of the process,

sufficient to introduce the structure of the proposal. We start this sketch by extracting from the birth of our current system the three keys to its success.

THE FORCES GUIDING OUR CURRENT SYSTEM

With respect to any school or system of schools, we can ask three basic questions: what brings it into being, what sustains it and what guides its daily activities? Answering these questions in different eras and contexts provides both a picture of schooling at that time and the reasons why schools have that form: for example, answering them for a community in agricultural colonial America generates a picture of schools such as the community Common School; answering them for industrial republican America generates the familiar picture of our current schools; answering them for 21st century postindustrial America generates the picture we need to re-engineer our schools.

Our prescription for designing a new system starts by answering these three basic question for our current system.

1. HOW DID OUR CURRENT SYSTEM ARISE?

We first need to understand what force or set of forces during the nineteenth century brought our current school system into being and maintained it for more than a century? The answer is frequently sought in social purposes, such as providing "an educated citizenry", an industrial workforce or well adjusted adults, but none of these goals spoke powerfully to average nineteenth (or twentieth) century Americans – they are the stuff of policy papers and books. The answer with the power to make everyone care about their schools aimed not at the head but at the heart, simultaneously appealing to self-interest and national identity: we know it as the desire for an equal opportunity society.

For almost a century Americans were able to see their public schools as distinctly American, reflecting the openness and classlessness of American society (contrasting sharply with European schools), and symbolizing optimistic belief in the future, providing a beacon of hope for a better life. We should look to this emotional and idealistic level to find the generative force of 21st century schools, and we will find it in the new and powerfully different sense that younger generations have of their role in society.

The historical power of the equal opportunity ideal cannot be overemphasized. It has affected virtually all aspects of the school system, from its gross design to the personal interactions in the classroom. For example, the curriculum is designed as an "educational ladder" allowing every student to progress from first grade to college entrance, and high stakes tests are designed to assess every student equally, with no biases. None of this works perfectly, but equal educational opportunity is one of the great principles shaping the current school system, and has contributed enormously to American society.

However, about thirty years ago progress in schooling stalled and the high school graduation rate leveled off at about seventy percent of students. Since then fewer and fewer educators have believed that we know how to push the graduation rate far above seventy percent: how to give that remaining thirty percent of students an equal opportunity to fulfill their dreams. Even fewer believed that we could achieve the goal of our recent national education strategy, No Child Left Behind, that every child would become proficient in English and Math by 2014. The doubters were, of course, proven correct.

Though still important, equal opportunity no longer plays the same energizing role that it did in the early twentieth century. Many urban students see little opportunity to escape their surroundings by studying hard at their local school, and many suburban students regard schooling as a right not a precious opportunity; often their goal is to get through school with high enough grades to avoid trouble. In large part, we seem to have settled into a routine acceptance of public schooling, having lost our early idealistic belief in its possibilities. Any new public school system will need to find and satisfy a powerful new public aspiration: one that upgrades and extends our commitment to equal educational opportunity

2. WHAT ORGANIZES AND SUSTAINS OUR CURRENT SCHOOL SYSTEM?

The second of our three basic questions asks what sustains such a large and complex system, but for our purposes we can ask the more precise question, "how did nineteenth century planners organize schools as a statewide or national enterprise?" Whether driven by such a conscious sense of planning or simply by commonsense, our nineteenth century ancestors answered the question by adopting the model sweeping through their commercial world, the industrial model of organization, which provided both the vision and the (only) practical means to build and organize a large-scale school system. In retrospect the choice seems obvious, but in developing statewide systems of uniform schooling they were taking on a massive challenge, requiring the full deployment of industrial management techniques, some of which were still in their infancy. The resulting school system was and is one of the great industrial enterprises of the last two hundred years, today employing over three million adults, serving fifty million students and costing over six hundred billion dollars per year (2017–18). As we wonder about our own ability to overcome similarly enormous re-engineering issues, we can draw confidence from their success.

The consequences of choosing to create an industrial school system were as widespread and far-reaching as those generated by the commitment to equal opportunity. In particular, one critical requirement for industrial success was the standardization of as many products and processes as possible, and this became the hallmark of our schools. As far as possible, text books, classrooms, teaching methods, and even teachers were to be as standardized and interchangeable as possible, and eventually this became not only an economic requirement but a desirable approach in its own right.

Industrialized schooling was both inevitable and appropriate for the basic needs of the nineteenth century, but two hundred years later we recognize there are fundamental conflicts built into the design that limit its ability to satisfy twenty-first century needs. In particular, the single most important element of schooling, the teacher-student relationship, is inherently human: neither teachers nor students come naturally standardized, ready to participate in an efficient industrial process. Consequently, when measured against modern standards, the balancing act between humanity and standardization required to make the system work frustrates and alienates both teachers and students. This conflict has been recognized in many other large organizations, and we can learn from these pioneering organizations how to adopt modern attitudes to workers and clients.

3. WHICH EDUCATIONAL IDEAS GUIDE DAILY SCHOOL ACTIVITY?

Having briefly looked at two of the forces shaping

our current schools, it is time to look at the third: the dominant nineteenth-century educational ideas. Though great educational debates flourished throughout the last two hundred years, teaching practice today differs modestly from the pattern established with the arrival of the printed text book five hundred years ago. We still predominantly have classes of students of a common age, learning a standard curriculum from a standard set of texts, progressing at the same rate month by month and year by year, and assessed by public competitive tests. So pervasive is this model that we can find it today in virtually every corner of the world, and evidence of it in archaeological sites dating to 3,000 BCE. Its remarkable ubiquity and permanence lead many people to regard it as the one natural way for large numbers of students to learn, and we forget that the process is filled with man-made assumptions and decisions.

One particular assumption flows from a very traditional view of society – a child learns predominantly by listening to nearby adults, absorbing knowledge into an unformed brain. This has been the assumption for millennia, but the outside world increasingly encroaches on this parent-child relationship, and for most of their school life modern children absorb a significant fraction of their knowledge and understanding of the world from diverse and unpredictable sources.

The specific nineteenth century educational assumption held that the majority of intellectual knowledge required for a good education could first be implanted into the heads of a large number of teachers, and then transferred to an even larger number of students. Neither part of that assumption remains true today. The challenge of training three million teachers to the required educational standard far outstrips our capacity and constitutes another fundamental flaw in the industrial model of schooling. We have consistently responded to this failure by exhortations to redouble our efforts, despite having no success in the past and little reason to expect success in the future. In the early days of our current system, when it catered primarily to students aged fourteen or less studying the 3R's, it may have been a plausible goal, but, as the system grew in size and complexity, success has, if anything, receded. In retrospect we should not be surprised - it violates a fundamental industrial guideline: the larger the number of workers to be trained, the simpler the work must be. It would be hard to find industrialists willing to stake their future on being able to train a workforce of three million people to carry out a challenging, highly individual task at the level implied by our aspirations for a "quality education".

The inevitable consequence of maintaining this overestimate of our training abilities is that the system finds its own level and shows us what is possible. Barring some fundamental new insight or tool, we have the level of teaching that we can reasonably expect and no exhortation to the contrary is going to change that. We need to design a high quality school system that does not require extraordinary levels of industrial training of teachers.

The second part of the nineteenth century educational assumption, that children come as blank slates to be written upon by teachers, has also never been true, but until recently the consequences were not obvious or significant. Today, we know that every child comes "pre-wired" for many physical and intellectual tasks and that children gain much of their knowledge of the world by interacting with it. The industrialized teaching approach fitted well with the blank slate model, but fails miserably when asked to deal individually with each student trying to learn by interacting with teachers and the Internet. Although we have much to understand about how people learn most effectively, it is already clear that turning every classroom into a rich learning environment that can adapt to each student's unique needs and history is vital, but it violates almost every premise of an industrial classroom.

Even at this gross level of observation, we can see that the role of the teacher must change. First, we will need to base this role on a realistic assessment of the intellectual knowledge likely to be part of a teacher's skills; second, we must replace the industrial classroom with a flexible learning environment, and fit the role of the teacher to that environment, not vice versa. This will lead to other vital gains, such as the rapid transfer of new research results into the classroom via the learning environment.

The role played by teachers is only one part of current educational philosophy that needs changing, but it suggests how completely we need to rethink the educational ideas guiding our schools. As we follow through the prescription, we shall find that basic educational elements, such as selecting the curriculum and testing students' learning will also need to be rethought.

ANOTHER KEY ELEMENT: STABILITY AND HARMONY

The more we examine the current school system the more we can see how three forces gave it a characteristic shape: a powerful aspiration for equal opportunity provided the sustaining energy and resources; the dominant enterprise model of the day gave it a specific organizational form at the largest and smallest scales; and the dominant learning model of the day determined how the classroom functioned.

However, before we can look at how to update these forces, we can learn one more lesson from how the current system functions, and in the process understand why it is so resistant to reform.

These three forces do not act independently; they reinforce each other in many different ways, making the system super-stable.

For example, the idea of equal opportunity was rapidly interpreted in the context of schools as equal schooling; namely schools offered fair schooling by offering everyone the same schooling. This interpretation fits completely with the industrial model and the classic educational methods used in the classroom. Having identical text books, schools, tests and teachers is the ideal approach required by all three forces, which work together to provide unyielding resistance to many changes. We see this interaction of the three forces when adapting to the needs of dyslexic students, which requires extra resources (economic impact), complicates class administration (organization impact), and often requires "unfair" allowances, such as extra test time (equal schooling impact). We also see it when trying to improve teaching: teachers with unique teaching practices, no matter how effective, do not easily transfer to other schools, are hard to replace and do not deliver equal schooling.

Beyond these practical consequences, the mutual reinforcement of ideas and forces has its biggest impact at the unconscious level, adding enormously to the sense that there is only one way to design and run a public school system, and from there it is a short step to seeing almost any significant change as a violation of some fundamental principle of public schooling. For example, some educators and parents viscerally reject experiments such as charter schools, seeing them as unequal and unfair, while some object to the perceived draining of funds from the public system. Practical problems become matters of principle, educational changes become economic issues, fairness beliefs affect curriculum and testing practices, in endless interconnected loops. Whether realistic or not this is a natural consequence of the interconnectedness of the system: any substantive change inevitably challenges one or more of the fundamental pillars of the system, and has to be rejected to maintain the integrity of the system. During a period when the system is satisfying the perceived needs of society, this leads to a welcome stability, but when the system is "failing" this stability becomes rigidity fighting reform.

As another part of this "natural" model, many people unconsciously accept that public schooling should function as an academic obstacle course, designed so that the "best" students are rewarded as winners and the others are relative failures, and from there it is an easy extrapolation to other beliefs: that vocational education is necessarily inferior to academic education and that tests should sort students rather than characterize what they know and can do. There are many ways in which people unconsciously buy into a nineteenth century view of schooling as natural and inevitable, and consequently resist desirable reforms.

While schools operated in a society operating with a compatible set of self-reinforcing ideas, our schools fitted harmoniously with it, but as society increasingly rejects uniformity, unrestrained industrialization and social survival of the fittest, our schools feel powerful pressures to change in ways that violate their basic structure. They experience too many special cases, too many overbearing parents and too few students who see school as an opportunity. Such stresses will ultimately lead to breakdowns of increasing severity, and eventually to the restructuring of schools to be more in line with modern American society.

To see how this will occur we follow the second and third steps of the prescription: to update each of the three most significant forces on schools and to interpret how these changes will cause schools to evolve. The following is a brief summary of how this plays out, preparing the ground for subsequent chapters, which offer detailed proposals.

UPDATING THE THREE FORCES

We are in the early stages of a major transition from an industrial society to a postindustrial society whose characteristics are evolving rapidly. Though these are the early stages, we can see already how the three major forces on schools are changing. This chapter sketches these changes, so that we can then begin to see how the new form of the three basic forces will shape the future school system.

Specifically we need to look at the modern counterpart to the industrial model of organization, to project how schools will need to organize themselves, and use that to look at broader issues such as funding.

We also need to understand how the social urge for Equal Opportunity can be reinterpreted for schools, giving them a new emotionally powerful role for the majority of Americans.

When we have a good understanding of how these two forces have evolved we will be in a better position to think about the evolution of our educational ideas.

UPDATING THE ORGANIZATIONAL MODEL: AN OVERVIEW

To describe an updated form of the industrial model of organization it helps to distinguish three characteristics of a large enterprise:

1. how it is organized on an enterprise scale;

2. how its individual groups function in relation to the overall enterprise

3. how its culture relates to surrounding society,

At each of these levels a modern large enterprise differs from a typical industrial organization. Briefly we can say:

1. At the enterprise level, large scale enterprises are evolving from hierarchical monoliths to dynamic networks, which often accommodate groups outside of the main enterprise, attaching and detaching them as required, including groups in foreign countries. Different levels of formal responsibility remain in the enterprise, but these are harder to pin down and actual responsibility flows to where the work is being done.

2. At the group level, and relative to past organizations, the groups comprising the network have a higher degree of independence, take more responsibility and must have higher levels of skill to perform well. These groups frequently negotiate clear goals - even contracts – to define their relationship with other groups in the enterprise; they

expect judgment by results and wide freedom in carrying out the work; they leverage other groups, both inside and outside of the enterprise, by exploiting the business and social/informal networks that are a fundamental part of their lives.

3. The Culture: modern enterprises function as a special form of normal life, without the distinct rigid codes of behavior that once characterized large scale industrial organizations, such as IBM or GM. The boundary between work and play is more porous and less geared to times of day; people frequently communicate with other workers from home, vacation and while traveling.

Taken together and applying them to the school system seen as a national or state enterprise, these shifts will change how schools need to function and will affect almost all practical details of school life: the responsibilities of superintendents, principals and teachers; the responsibilities and funding of schools; even the legal status of schools. The demands on principals and teachers will increase significantly, offset by more flexibility in achieving goals. The relationship between schools and parents will also change, as will the economics of dealing with varying parental demands. Each student will have a personal learning environment, which will be networked with several schools and learning centers, taking advantage of learning coaches, family members and peers to support a personal learning plan.

These are some of the organizational changes that will be stimulated by a new economic context, and in a later chapter, we will present the specific organization that we believe flows naturally from interpreting the new school system as a modern large enterprise - just as nineteenth century educators saw their new school system as a form of the industrial enterprise.

UPDATING EQUAL OPPORTUNITY: AN OVERVIEW

For an industrial society to function effectively people naturally identify themselves as members of groups: corporate employees, professionals, consumers, trade unionists, students, scouts, and many others. This arises naturally as a human form of industrial standardization, enabling people to fit themselves into the artificial slots so important to the industrial model. By fitting in, individuals benefit from the power of the group, but at the cost of tailoring their needs to the common denominator. Increasingly today, people reject this compromise and demand more individual attention: as consumers, as patients, as workers, as students and as members of many erstwhile monolithic groups.

A particularly relevant example is occurring within the group of students, namely the growth in the number of special education students. Experts estimate that anywhere from ten to twenty percent of students require some form of special treatment to read and write fluently, and beyond that specific set of skills the list of special needs can be extended almost indefinitely; we feel the need to create subgroups of students with labels such as ADHD, autistic, depressed, gifted, and eventually to distinguish between the learning needs of boys and girls. According to the equal approach to schooling, these are deficits, which ideally should not have to be taken into account, but increasingly parents demand individual attention for their children. These parents are raising the bar, and overturning the assumption that we can treat all students as if they were the same, and it is no longer acceptable for schools to treat individual differences as deficits from an assumed standard student. Many parents are telling us that nineteenth century standards and attitudes are no longer good enough.

How does this shift to individuality affect our interpretation of Equal Opportunity in schools? The interpretation for the industrial era was that equal educational opportunity meant an equal school experience for every student, but from our modern vantage point we recognize that equal schooling has never been fair schooling, because every child starts with a different set of requirements. Equal schooling implies selecting one particular way of schooling and applying it uniformly, with obvious benefit to those children who closely suit that way of learning. When the challenge was to provide large numbers of children with a basic education, the uniform approach was fair enough, and provided such enormous benefits as to overwhelm any objections to its lack of fairness. But it fails to meet the demands of the twenty-first century, and leaves many parents feeling that schools do not care about their particular needs. We need to raise the bar and try to provide students with the best education for them individually - that is the true meaning of fairness in schooling.

This shift, to providing fair educational opportunity by treating every student as an individual, is too profound to be bolted onto the current framework – it violates too many educational instincts and practices. It also risks becoming another element of the school mission statement, to be used on special occasions. We need instead to carry into the heart of schools the educational equivalent of the social shift towards individuality, and to do that it helps to distinguish four elements of the social shift:

A shift in power from supplier to customers: a modern Henry Ford asks customers for their color preferences and tries to deliver them.

A shift in personal identity: an emotional shift that speaks to a deep need for the individual to emerge from group conformity.

A shift in technology: one that enables highly dynamic group participation; that expands our ability to publicize personal characteristics; that vastly increases an individual's power to influence society.

A shift in capability: that places knowledge skills at the heart of adult success, and requires each individual to control how they acquire those skills.

Combined, these create a different way to look at our current society compared to centuries past, and they partially characterize what we mean by a postindustrial society. In agricultural societies people fit into preordained "stations in life" according to a Divine Plan. In industrial societies people fit themselves into slots created by the needs of the industrial process; people can make choices, but from a limited set of options. In a postindustrial society people have innumerable choices and can experiment with different ways of being in society, but to do so they have to be skilled at using the expanded mechanisms offered, and be more responsible and entrepreneurial. To prepare students for this complex world requires a new definition of fairness in education, one that replaces equality with something more complex.

A fair education for a postindustrial society has to help each child achieve their own best way of preparing for this postindustrial world, not dictate to them what is in their best interests. Exercising personal responsibility in adult life cannot be learned in schools that unilaterally define success, determine the tests, insist on one curriculum and treat students and parents as transitory passive elements of the system. A school must function similarly to the rest of society, so that students learn naturally how to function in real life. This shift is so profound that it requires a redefinition of the role of schools: a school must become a service, and treat students and parents as clients.

UPDATING OUR EDUCATIONAL IDEAS: AN OVERVIEW

Before attempting to understand how the third force - our collection of educational ideas - needs to evolve, it helps to notice something that did not happen in parallel with the nineteenth century social and economic changes: there was no dramatic change in the basic educational ideas or practices in the transition from colonial schools to public schools. Attempts, such as "child centered" schooling, made very little long term impact, and despite noisy debates, curriculum ideas and teaching practices remained remarkably similar to those existing prior to the nineteenth century. Why did one of the three pillars of the school system not undergo radical change in parallel with the other two?

The first reason harks back to the need for stability, as expressed in the self reinforcing nature of the three pillars. Only those changes in educational practices that were compatible with the industrial model and the equal schooling interpretation of equal opportunity could survive and flourish. The classical practices fitted almost perfectly while many of the proposed variations did not.

The second reason opens a fruitful line of thinking about the present situation, and it will be developed more fully in Chapter 5: Technology the Great Enabler. The central idea is to look at schools as training institutions in the technology of knowledge, just as we might look at an institution for training people in agricultural or transportation technology, and to look at schools that way we first need to look at the basic idea of a knowledge technology.

A knowledge technology enhances our biological abilities to create and manipulate knowledge, to remember it and to communicate it. The one pervasive knowledge technology we have created in the last five thousand years is Writing - the use of "paper and pencil", and much of the basic 3R's curriculum covers how to use that technology: how to encode data (write) and decode data (read); how to create documents using the correct punctuation and other conventions; how to store and retrieve large amounts of knowledge, how to communicate knowledge in written form: in short, to master our basic knowledge technology. The truly academic part of the curriculum teaches students more advanced ways to exploit this technology.

Seeing schools as institutions for the training of our one knowledge technology suggests why teaching did not change radically at the birth of our current school system. Since the fundamentals of this pervasive knowledge technology did not change during the nineteenth century, there was no need to change the core practices of teaching it, except where the demands of industrialization and social needs required changes. This situation continues in schools today, and is a powerful reason why digital technologies have had so little impact on the classroom. They are viewed as a way to help teach the established knowledge technology – reading/writing – and, as such, are used only where they fit in and add value. Computers are used mostly as extensions of previous technologies, such as radio, TV, and overhead projectors, none of which had a significant impact on classroom practice.

The fundamental revolution in the classroom will occur when schools decide that a new knowledge technology is rapidly replacing reading/writing as the dominant knowledge technology, and that its mastery has become the more important skill for students. This transition is well underway outside of schools, and we need a thoughtful way to adapt the curriculum to prepare students for this new world. The challenge goes far beyond keyboard skills and searching the Internet and it is driven by a major shift in how knowledge is created, represented, communicated, and authenticated. Knowledge technology Version 2 has arrived and will rapidly replace Version 1 (reading/writing), and just as schools were created to teach Version 1, so they will need to be re-created to teach Version 2.

In tandem with this change to the core of schooling, we need to deal with a critical failure point buried in the industrial system model for schools. Quality teaching is a craft: it relies on the individual skills and personality of the teacher; it builds on the unique attributes of the students; and it finds success in unpredictable events, such as "teachable moments." At its most critical point, the current school system has a craft embedded in an industrial system, thereby creating a bottleneck that throttles attempts at major change down to those that fit the craft model of teaching: for example, changes that do not require the re-education of three million teachers.

This failure point has resulted in very small gains in the single most important measure of teaching effectiveness – how well children learn in any given period. Most of the gains of the last two hundred years have come in activities at the periphery of teaching, but not in the heart of the process; text books can be printed more efficiently, worksheets can be copied and classes scheduled with less teacher effort, but as every study observes, the crucial factor in school performance is still the individual teacher.

In a world demanding far more knowledge for successful self-expression, this stagnation in learning effectiveness is unacceptable, and points to the need to rethink how students should learn in schools. After five thousand years of using essentially the same techniques to help students to learn, we need to create a new teaching/learning model with at least one essential new feature: it must encourage and enable constant improvement in the learning process. From examining situations other than schooling, we know some of the features of such an environment: it must be research driven and supported by technology; it must have a culture of change, not of tradition; it must be organizationally flexible and capable of adapting to ideas from outside of the system and to local conditions; and the emphasis must be on the learner, not the teacher. Some of these attributes are built into this proposal as part of the system's design, but the specific process of using a nationally funded research program to feed new learning approaches into schools will need careful additional work.

Today we lack the knowledge to design this far more effective learning environment, but we cannot afford to wait until we have all the answers. Instead we can start by creating a system that can improve constantly, and which has the clear goal to search out technologies that can help.

Updating our educational ideas to create a new school system will need to proceed along two parallel paths. Some basic changes will be required by our new sense of fairness in learning - adapting the path of learning to the individual. These we build into the structure from the beginning and are outlined in later chapters. Other changes will come because we now recognize how little we understand about learning, and how important it is to create learning environments that themselves adapt and learn. The new learning environments will be research driven, technologically sophisticated and highly professional.

STABILITY AND THE
THREE MODERN FORCES

There are many ways in which the new social, economic

and educational forces will interact to provide stability to the future school system. As we develop more of the details of the proposed school system, we draw repeatedly on this principle of self-reinforcement to select, from the possible ways to organize a school, those which "naturally" fit with the fundamental principles and forces shaping the system. The result is very different from our current system, but is equally natural if we see it as part of our future, rather than our past.

The need for fundamental change becomes stronger every day, but how do we go about creating a new system? Many good ideas have been tried over the last few decades, with very little impact on the key parameters: the speed or depth of learning of the majority of students. We now sketch a way to think about this design problem, one that holds the promise of avoiding faddish thinking while embracing radically new ideas.

DESIGNING A NEW SCHOOL SYSTEM: AN OVERVIEW

Having experienced thirty years of failed attempts to reform our current school system, it is tempting to conclude that it is a hopeless task, doomed to further failures by politics, tradition and sheer complexity. However we can now see that the current system is designed to resist change, and the correct deduction from the failures of the past is that we need a complete redesign, not a reform of the current design. If we took each of the ideas proposed in later chapters and tried to graft them onto the current system, they would fail as miserably as all the other reforms.

We have also learned that the core ideas must be embedded in the fabric of the system, informing major political decisions as well as daily classroom practice. A system as complex as a national school system cannot be managed from the top. Many decisions are taken daily in each school and classroom: in each hiring decision, curriculum decision, testing decision and in a wider context in each PTA meeting. Consequently the system must be designed so that individuals are led to make the appropriate decisions naturally. There must be a culture, a set of priorities and an organization that directly supports appropriate decision-making. All great organizations have this characteristic, whether acting commercially, such as Apple, or militarily, such as the Navy Seals or religiously, such as a monastery. Where there is a culture of honesty people will act predominantly honestly: where there is a culture of greed, they will act greedily and in their self-interest.

We use this idea repeatedly in creating a new design for a school system. Many crucial design issues can be resolved by appealing to the core ideas and the spirit motivating the design, and the result is often the opposite of current thinking. This is not change for the sake of being different, but an attempt to create a learning environment that is consistent and appealing to students, teachers and parents: one that fulfills powerfully felt ambitions and aspirations.

However, we must also accept that many decisions cannot and should not be taken now, nor cast in stone for decades to come. Modern organizations are created and guided with the knowledge that change is necessary and desirable, and the management of that change must also be embedded in the core design of the enterprise. The key to success lies in establishing very firm basic guidelines and encouraging individual responsibility to makes changes within those guidelines.

With these ideas in mind, we can map an approach to designing a new school system, using the three elements we have discussed earlier.

1. Equal Opportunity in public schools will be reinterpreted as individual schooling, satisfying the growing need for people to express their individuality;

2. Industrial management of schools will give way to the new dynamic network model of large enterprises;

3. The educational focus will shift from students attending schools to schools servicing students and their learning needs; also,

- the core intellectual goal will shift from mastering Knowledge Technology Version 1 (i.e. reading and writing) to Knowledge Technology Version 2. (See Chapter 5 for a description of this new Knowledge Technology.)

Elaborating each of these three ideas constitutes the three major sections of the book.

Chapter 2, "Equal Opportunity Revisited" addresses the question of how to express a commitment to individuality in education, and how to embed it into the core of the school system. It is a profound change, deserving a quasi constitutional anchoring of this new national sense of education, and we turn to history for clues how to capture and sustain this new role for education.

Chapter 3, "The School System Reorganized" deals with the legal, financial and operational structure of the system. The comparable design decisions taken more than one hundred years ago had the widest possible affect on our current schools – for example, using local property taxes as a major source of financial support - and similarly powerful consequences flow from the decisions to use the new dynamic network model of large enterprises;

Chapter 4, "The Classroom Redefined" proposes radically different ways to define the curriculum, to generate standards and to assess students against them; it also proposes a fundamentally new role for teachers and students. Most of these changes are driven either by the needs of the social and economic changes, or by the need to raise substantially and continuously the performance of teachers and students. The focus is on structural changes, leaving important specifics to individual schools and teachers.

Due to its special significance, Chapter 5 addresses how technology changes knowledge, tracing the history of writing as Version 1 of our knowledge technology and clarifies some of the important differences between Version 1 and Version 2 of that technology. The comparison provides a basis for suggesting how technology will play a different role in future classrooms.

Throughout the rest of this book we use the term "*fmf* schools" as a shorthand for schools based upon the ideas proposed here. There are approximately fifty million students in our public schools, and the title reminds us of that fact and how much is at stake:

fmf .... *f*ifty million *f*utures

2.
EQUAL OPPORTUNITY REVISITED

One of the major motivating forces guiding the public school system has been its commitment to equal opportunity, and the public has rewarded this commitment with longstanding and deep support. Any new public school system must find a way to continue this commitment, and retain public support.

Throughout the last 150 years we have pursued an implementation of equal opportunity that made sense when the goal was to lift the large majority of children from near illiteracy to a level adequate for participation in a flourishing industrial workforce, while providing a small but important percentage of children the opportunity to go to college, if they were academically successful. In this implementation the equal opportunity is provided in the form of equal schooling: as far as possible we want every child to have comparable teachers, classrooms, text books, curriculum, tests, facilities and computers, and to pass through the system in age cohorts, ready to graduate as a peer group at the same time. It is a fair approach in the sense that each student is (in theory) presented with the same challenges and opportunities, and (in theory) success will go to the most academically capable. We have come to see this as the natural implementation of equal opportunity, and one that emphasizes merit over privilege. However, this implementation needs rethinking, for both social and educational reasons. Here we pursue the social component and defer the educational discussion to Chapter 4: The Classroom Revisited.

Our current concept of social equal opportunity is much more refined and personal than the group oriented visions of our industrial forefathers. Today we demand to be treated as an individual as well as a member of the community or other groups. In the recent Industrial Age, individuals submerged parts of their identity in corporations, in unions, in large political parties and in other groups, all of which enhanced their power in society. Around the world this trend is reversing and people are asking and being asked to act more independently, to take more responsibility and to recover some of their individuality, whether as worker, consumer, patient or citizen.

We have come to realize that fair treatment is often not the same as equal treatment, that good service is not the same as equal service, and that a good education is not the same as an equal education. A striking current example can be found in voter registration laws that require id cards that are much less available to some segments of the population, and pose an unfair burden on poor people. This is an equal but unfair requirement. Also, as parents we realize that our children cannot be trained to be independent adults by spending twelve years in an institution founded on the belief that ideally all children should be treated as if they were the same.

In short, we are in the process of finding a new equilibrium between our role as individuals and our role as members of society, and our public schools will need to support that new equilibrium and function compatibly with it.

However, the belief in equal schooling permeates our thinking about education, and almost every aspect of schools, and we can only create a new school system with the more refined implementation of equal opportunity as individual schooling, if we create a powerful new emotional and social goal for schools. That is the purpose of this chapter.

THE NEW SOCIAL COMPACT

We are looking for a way to provide an emotional appeal to the public and a practical guide to educators, emphasizing the new desire to enhance our lives as individuals within the community. The Founding Fathers were faced with a similar challenge in creating powerful beacons for the newly emerging republic, and one of the tools they used was to declare that people had natural rights that had previously been ignored.

We shall take the same approach, and create a new Social Compact, between the individual and society, regarding our education.

THE NEW SOCIAL COMPACT FOR LEARNING

All People have:

The natural right to pursue their own learning.

A right to a fair allocation of society's resources to support their learning.

The responsibility to learn how to be an effective citizen.

We will expand on the interpretation of this declaration, but two points are worth emphasizing immediately.

The *natural right to pursue their own learning* means that we start from the assumption that students (together with parents) control all aspects of their schooling, and we should only restrict that student control where there are compelling reasons to do so. While this may seem extreme it is both logical and practical, as we will see shortly.

Secondly, this compact is to be interpreted as powerfully and completely as we currently interpret the idea of equal schooling: namely, it will govern every design decision and all aspects of daily life in *fmf* schools. Throughout this chapter and the subsequent working out of the organizational and educational aspects of the design, we shall appeal to this compact to decide many key issues.

The remainder of this chapter is devoted to fleshing out how we intend this compact to be interpreted.

NATURAL RIGHTS

A natural right is a right we possess when we are born, independently of our circumstances, our behavior or any other contingency. In principle it exists independently of the society around us, and would, for example, exist if we were born on a desert island. In particular we do not have to justify its existence, nor accept that our previous failure to observe it mitigates invoking it now. We simply assert that in the 21st century it is vital to the happiness of the individual and to the ultimate success of our society that we protect and promote this right.

The particular right covers all aspects of our learning, no matter where or when it occurs, whether it is formal or informal learning, or whether we learn alone or with a teacher's support. We do not have to prove that we have the right. We are presumed to have it, and anyone wishing to abrogate or restrict it must have compelling reasons. However, all rights are likely to come into conflict with other rights, and society has to strike a balance between them, using the political process. The balance point changes over time as society evolves.

Associated with this natural right are derived rights, which differ from a natural right by depending on society for their meaning. A common example is the difference between the right to freedom and the right to habeas corpus: the first is a natural right, while the second only exists in the context of society, and describes a way in which our natural right to freedom is protected. We shall be less concerned with these derived rights, assuming that they will be defined as needed to ensure the appropriate application of the basic right.

Skeptics often challenge the value of declaring powerful rights, on the grounds of impracticality, asserting, for example, that we cannot possibly allow everyone to determine their own learning, especially in a public school system, and that it is totally uneconomic and will lead to chaos. But the same argument applied to the right to pursue happiness, especially in a time when for many people life was "solitary, poor, nasty, brutish and short." Rights do not have to be immediately practical; they arise from a belief that they are "natural", and their role is to provide a beacon. They define an aspiration for how we would like the world to be, knowing that we can never fully achieve that utopian state. In the Social Compact we are saying that we aspire to a world in which all people have complete control over their learning, and we will work diligently towards it.

THE RIGHT TO A FAIR ALLOCATION OF SOCIETY'S RESOURCES

We increasingly recognize that possessing a right without the means to give it practical expression is an empty promise. Fortunately the right to a fair allocation of society's resources for an education has been both practically and, in most States, constitutionally established for many years. This makes moral and practical sense to most people. Morally it provides the platform for equal opportunity, and practically it is an investment in the future health and well-being of society. These reasons are even more compelling now, since we are entering a knowledge based society, in which citizens are completely dependent on their ability to use knowledge.

Some people may feel that society should not pay for education without controlling very carefully how that money is spent, but, for the moral and practical reasons given above, simply cutting off funding for self-directed education would be very short sighted. We already have other instances of public financing without detailed control of how the money is used; we do not require detailed control of how college students spend their time or how people spend their Social Security money, for example. But the Social Compact does not advocate totally free spending of our personal educational resources. The Compact operates within a framework established by each State, which controls certain elements of public schooling, though far fewer elements than today. The details are spelled out in Chapters 3 and 4.

THE RESPONSIBILITY TO LEARN HOW TO BE AN EFFECTIVE CITIZEN

Rights typically come with responsibilities, and in the Social Compact one responsibility is spelled out explicitly. We all have a responsibility to try to become sufficiently educated to function effectively in society, even if we choose not to participate fully. Children have the responsibility to prepare themselves in several ways for their future role in society: to be able to work and not be an economic burden on society; to be able to understand and vote on major issues; to be able to understand and obey laws, and in general to participate at least minimally in civic life.

Beyond this, society has a compelling interest in those attitudes of citizens that affect its stability and capability to function smoothly. Although State sponsored molding of attitudes is a politically fraught area, schools have always had this involvement in inculcating social "manners", and have always attracted controversy as a result.

fmf schools have a particular responsibility to educate students in those social attitudes that balance the increasing tendency to emphasize personal needs above society's needs, and the curriculum has an important Civics component explicitly designed to educate students in their future role as citizens.

STUDENTS RIGHTS AND PARENTS RIGHTS

Since we are born with natural rights, a strict interpretation of the Social Compact suggests that from the earliest years children should decide whether or not to go to school: a conclusion that evokes both horror and ridicule, and is not the intention of this proposal. Since society typically defines the age at which significant responsibility passes from parents to children, as 18 years, the implication is that school students play little role in deciding their own educational path, but there are important reasons to focus on the student and leave the parent in the background.

As a matter of rights, parents have no explicit

constitutional right to control their children's schooling (and historically sometimes had to be compelled to send their children to school), but *fmf* schools need and welcome strong parental involvement. The assumption in this proposal is that parents will continue to have legal control over their children's education, and will take many of the decisions determining how that education evolves. In this proposal we sometimes reinforce that assumption by referring to the *student/parent* as a combined entity, leaving unsaid how the family reaches a decision. The organization of *fmf* schools accommodates most family arrangements for balancing the rights of children and parents, with one proviso; neither right should completely vanquish the other and, where there is doubt, the interests of the child are paramount.

In terms of designing the *fmf* school system, we apply the following principles:

I. Schools and teachers have an explicit requirement to encourage students to take responsibility for their own learning;

II. Schools are NOT ultimately responsible for the educational success of any student;

III. Most elements of the system are designed as if the student/parents have ultimate control, with a few explicit exceptions;

IV. Students should be seriously consulted on all decisions concerning their learning.

As an example of how these principles are applied, the pedagogy and curriculum are constructed to support the explicit goal to teach all students how to take responsibility for their learning, so that by the time they leave school they are ready to become effective life long learners. Teaching this learning skill is as much part of the curriculum as teaching math. *fmf* schools can only succeed at teaching this skill if teachers visibly respect students, which implies consulting them appropriately. This is one of several attitudes that permeate *fmf* Schools and are probably never mentioned explicitly, just as current schools have implicit attitudes to students. Parents are encouraged to take a similar attitude towards their children's learning.

THE CHALLENGE OF TAKING RESPONSIBILITY

One of the apparent advantages of the current system in which schools are responsible for a student's education is that it evens the playing field between those students with parents knowledgeable and aggressive enough to make demands, and those parents who through ignorance or sheer lack of time cannot. However that has the significant disadvantage of encouraging the mentality of dropping children off at school and expecting teachers to do the rest. In a very real sense, parents today believe that it is the teachers' or schools' fault if a student does not perform as expected.

In the *fmf* system, the balance is shifted, but great attention is paid to motivating and assisting the student/parents to play their proper role. For example, as described later, the school system is designed as a SERVICE, and one of its major services is to advise and guide student/parents in their choices throughout their school careers. In many cases student/parents will find a school that they trust and then mostly follow the advice of that school for most educational decisions.

However, schools are not perfect and student/parents will sometimes need independent advice and this is provided on a continuing basis by Learning Councillors in the newly proposed *fmf* Learning Centers (see Chapter 3), which are independent of any individual school.

THE CONSTITUTIONAL ISSUE

One thorny issue has been, and will be, left unresolved – whether this right to manage our own learning should be constitutionally established. When, during the Depression, FDR faced the same issue with respect to peoples' right to a minimum of economic security, he decided against trying to establish the right constitutionally, preferring to establish it as a de facto right by passing specific laws, but not trying to establish the general principle. Scholars and politicians continue to argue whether this was a fully successful strategy, and whether within a legally enforceable constitution such as ours it is even practical to have such a broad economically demanding right.

In our case, the point is moot, until there is sufficient demand from the American people for political recognition of the Social Compact. Our current public school system functions well without the principle of Equal Educational Opportunity being fully established constitutionally, and *fmf* schools may well follow a similar path. However, whatever its legal status, the Social Compact guides everything about *fmf* schools.

IN BRIEF

History has shown us that a public school system must satisfy a deep emotional national need, and one that fits with the current enduring sense of how "we, the people" see ourselves. As we move from an industrial age, geared to the efficient functioning of large groups, to an Internet age, geared to the individual, we need to re-examine our concept of Fairness in education. We can no longer equate it with Equal Schooling. We must now strive for the higher goal of giving each student the education best suited to the detailed circumstances, capabilities and aspirations of that student/parent.

However, that new higher aspiration cannot be bolted onto the existing system that explicitly rejects too much adaptation to the individual: it must be placed at the heart of the new system and inform every decision, at all times and in all places: in the design of the system, and in the daily decisions made in each school.

Such a change can only be carried through if we elevate it to a national aspiration, and using the inspiration of the Founding Fathers, we propose a new Social Compact:

THE NEW SOCIAL COMPACT FOR LEARNING

All People have:

The natural right to pursue their own learning.

A right to a fair allocation of society's resources to support their learning.

The responsibility to learn how to be an effective citizen.

The effect of this Compact is to radically shift the responsibility for an individual's education from the state to the individual, aided by the parent(s). This is appropriate in the Internet Age, when the acquisition of knowledge is one of the most significant determinants of success and the ability to pursue happiness.

This is a bold step sharing the same commitment to trust "the people" as was shown in setting up the Republic, over two hundred years ago, and the same arguments of impracticality and irresponsibility will be raised. But we have learned that, with the right structure to support and guide them, "the people" are surprisingly adept at managing their own affairs while maintaining a commitment to the common good.

However, we cannot simply shift the responsibility while leaving the same tools and attitudes in place. It is a challenging responsibility to become a lifelong learner, to recognize the importance of having the appropriate knowledge skills and to know how to get them. The *fmf* school system must proactively teach *student/ parents* these values and how to acquire the skills. The curriculum includes specific elements to support this new responsibility, and teachers accept as one of their main roles the coaching of students to learn how to learn.

The right of all student/parents to manage their own schooling is built into all of the following detailed proposals for an *fmf* school system. It radically alters most of its major characteristics, compared to today.

3.
THE SCHOOL SYSTEM REORGANIZED

How a school system is organized determines much of the learning environment and much of the economic effectiveness of the schools, and it is vital to have an organization matching the style of contemporary society, drawing on the best ideas from the commercial world, and creating an environment that prepares students for that world, and for one that matches their social world outside school. Gone are the days when we can afford to create an artificial school world significantly out of step with the surrounding real world.

Many large commercial enterprises are evolving their structures into dynamic intelligent networks, dismantling many of the more rigid hierarchical structures that served them well as industrial enterprises. The reasons are straightforward and apply equally to schools:

I. Many problems and opportunities are best handled by the people close to the situation, not in a predetermined part of a hierarchy;

II. Distributing responsibility maximizes the use of all of the intelligence in the organization, offering a potentially large gain in effectiveness;

III. Employees feel more valued, and are more inclined to make their best contribution;

IV. Local employees can understand and respond better to changing local circumstances;

V. Resources can be co-opted and released more quickly, allowing greater access to expensive resources.

Our schools desperately need to innovate and find ways to increase the learning capacity of our students by much more than an occasional percentage point. To do so they need to experiment, to incorporate tools and ideas from anywhere, and to continuously take advantage of the latest research. Only by adopting a flexible network structure can this be achieved today.

However stability has a role to play, and above all the organization needs a steady and inspiring sense of purpose to offset the continuous change; this guiding, stabilizing purpose is provided by the Social Compact, and the commitment to move closer and closer to providing each student with individually tailored support. As we now look at the various components of the *fmf* school system, we will see how the Social Compact acts as a glue forming the parts into a whole.

THE ELEMENTS OF THE FMF SCHOOL SYSTEM

It would be wrong to paint too detailed a picture of the *fmf* School system; too much will depend on political decisions and the environment in which it is launched, and doing so violates the spirit of the design, which encourages local adaptation and control of many details. However, since flexibility can only make sense within a structure that is clear and not readily modified, it is important for us to propose a macro structure.

To provide that structure we describe certain characteristics of the following elements of the *fmf* school system.

1. The State:
2. The System:
3. An *fmf* School:
4. Teachers:
5. Students:
6. Funding:

Although many of the following details have been chosen as the best way to implement the intent of the New Social Compact, there is clearly a level of arbitrariness and selectivity involved. We have tried to focus on those issues that either distinguish the *fmf* approach or which suggest how the system would work in practice. Ultimately a system as complex as a public school system will result from many compromises, which may diminish the power of the approach as well as improve it.

Before we start the description, it is worth reminding ourselves that this is a proposal for a PUBLIC school system, even though some aspects of it do not satisfy our current interpretation of that term. It is public in the sense that its purpose is a public purpose, intended to improve society by advancing the knowledge and wisdom of its citizens; it is under the ultimate control of the State, which places certain specific demands on all schools, and it is funded publicly.

1. THE ROLE OF THE STATE

The State (interpreted as each State or the Federal Government, according to the political environment of the time) plays a role similar to today's role with one important exception - it does not operate schools or set most of the educational rules. There are two major reasons for this change:

I. It is vital that there is a political entity capable of independently judging and reporting on the effectiveness of our schools, without being encumbered with the need to justify that effectiveness. There is ample evidence today of the loss of objectivity due to combining political control with operational responsibility. The State should have political control, but limited operational responsibility.

II. Centralized management of schools can no longer deal with the complexity of schooling, but State operation is incompatible with highly distributed management of the kind proposed here. A key reason for this is risk: politically accountable management naturally attempts to minimize the risks of failure and usually does not support local risk taking, experimentation and adaptation.

We, the public, exacerbate the situation by trying to affect detailed educational decisions through the political process.

The separation of political control from operational management has been a cornerstone of our overall government since the beginning of the Republic; giving up that separation of powers for the public school system made sense when it could be assumed that schooling was mostly commonsense, and that it was vital to have central State enforcement of equal schooling. Today we have the opposite situation - schooling is a complex professional activity that requires fair but differentiated treatment of each student.

In this proposal, the primary responsibility of the State is to set the rules under which students, parents and professional educators can negotiate individual interpretations of a fair allocation and use of resources in support of each student's education. Even without State operational control, there will be many such rules; here we focus on those that affect the overall shape of the system.

I. The State determines the meaning of a "fair allocation of educational resources." This is a political decision outside of the scope of this proposal;
II. The State provides the funding and the system for distributing it;
III. The State defines and enforces rules to guarantee the health and safety of the students and educators;
IV. The State controls the accreditation of every school;
V. The State defines and oversees audits of every school.
VI. The State steps in when the system is failing to provide a minimally satisfactory level of education to any group of students.
VII. The State defines a core part of the curriculum designed to give every student the minimum level of skill to function in society.

In a very meaningful sense, a school system is a market in which students, parents and school staff interact to help students to learn. The rules governing any market essentially determine its success or failure, and we will need to pay careful attention to the details of the rules laid down by States in governing their educational "markets". More insight into the intended rules will come from the remaining parts of the proposal, but we should note immediately that the term "market" does not imply profit or money as the determining factor. or measurement.

2. THE FMF SCHOOL SYSTEM

By any standard the US public school system is a large enterprise, having over three million employees and servicing over fifty million students each year; its budget is close to half a trillion dollars (2018). It needs to be a shining example of a large 21st century enterprise, employing the best organizational and management techniques, and all signs point to the dynamic network model of organization as the preferred and most effective choice for most modern enterprises. The stimulus is coming from the success of smaller organizations, but large enterprises are increasingly adapting and adopting the network model.

The *fmf* School System is based on the dynamic

network model of organization, with the following components:

I. The national system is physically an interconnected set of State systems, each of which is its own network:

   a. Each of these physical networks is a Virtual Private Network providing controlled access, while using predominantly commercial infrastructure;

   b. Other networks, such as university networks, have controlled access to parts of the school network;

   c. The infrastructure is operated and maintained by the State Department of Education (DoE) as a service to all schools;

II. The State DoE supplies certain key services:

   a. Registering and tracking all certified schools in the State;

   b. Registering and tracking all school-age children in the State, including which schools they are currently attending;

   c. Managing and tracking the distribution of funds to students and schools;

   d. Financing and organizing major capital expenditures; Legal services; Fee based bulk procurement services, such as insurance, health, computers, etc.;

III. Data gathering and publishing, and statistical testing.

IV. The State or a community will frequently own and lease to schools space or other facilities.

V. External Resources: individual schools make extensive use of resources external to the school system, whether these are private, commercial, public, educational or open. These resources grow around the school systems (national and State specific resources) and are connected as required.

3. AN INDIVIDUAL FMF SCHOOL

An *fmf* school is the primary node in the school network, and its relationship to the State DoE and to the student/parents is very different from current schools. The goal is to give each school a high degree of independence and a high degree of responsibility, while the task of the DoE is to provide services to the schools, and oversee them without significantly interfering.

The major characteristics of an *fmf* School:

I. An *fmf* school is legally a not-for-profit:
   a. The operators of a school must have their primary allegiance to the students, not to shareholders.

II. An *fmf* school is run by a Principal and a Board
   a. The Principal has the authority to hire, fire, organize and direct the school within the framework established by the Board
   b. The Board functions as a typical not-for-profit Board: e.g. it hires the Principal

III. An *fmf* school is Certified and Audited by the Department of Education
   a. Every year the school must arrange and pay for an independent audit that certifies its compliance with its Department of Education standards;
   b. The topics are mostly non-educational, but include data on staff and facilities;
   c. The audit results must be given to all parents and prospective parents;
   d. The Department of Education can require the school to close temporarily or permanently if the audit indicates dangerous or extensive failures;
   e. A school can appeal the results of an audit;

IV. An *fmf* school supplies a Professional Service
   a. Providing guidance to student/parents on possible learning paths to reach the student's objectives;
   b. Providing diagnostic services on a

student's competence and learning characteristics;

c. Providing a professional learning environment of tools and teachers

d. According to a contract agreed with student/parents prior to attendance at the school;

V. This Service is a Value-Added Service

a. The school proposes to help a student progress from the student's current level to an agreed next level of learning;

b. Each student has a separate plan;

c. Failure of the student to stick to the contract (e.g. do specified homework) invalidates the contract;

d. The service is typically expressed as assisting students to gain various certificates;

e. There will be State mandated "packages" - e.g. elementary schools must offer the complete elementary curriculum;

f. "High schools" can offer more specialized services - e.g. languages or sciences or liberal arts;

VI. Enrollment

a. The school specifies publicly the criteria for acceptance (including complying with legal anti-bias laws)

b. The school must accept all who satisfy the criteria or must have a lottery if oversubscribed;

c. The school must continue to keep enrolled any student who maintains the terms of the contract;

It is worth emphasizing points IV and V. Each *fmf* school provides a value-added service to its clients, the students and the parents. It helps each client to formulate effective and realistic goals and to map out a plan to achieve those goals. The goals are always to help a student move from their current knowledge level to a new level: that is the meaning of the term "value-added". The plan proposes courses and learning plans with appropriate checkpoints, covering a single year or several years, and before starting the student/parent and school sign a contract spelling out the agreement. It is a serious educational and legal document that is designed to focus teachers and students on what they are trying to achieve. The responsibility of the school is to provide the specified services, and the responsibility of the student is to attend, and do the work proposed by the school. Provided the school supplies the services effectively, the responsibility for success lies with the student /parent.

The *fmf* School System makes a fundamental distinction between the school and the school building and any associated community functions. A school is the human and logical entity that focuses on students' learning; it can use any appropriate building, which may or may not have many of the facilities of a large current school; it can supply ancillary services if the staff decide that those facilities contribute to students' learning.

But it has one fundamental responsibility that must imbue its staff and its space: it must represent the power and opportunity of learning and knowledge; it must be organized as a center of learning; it must demonstrate what it means to be an effective student of learning. When students enter an *fmf* school, they must know and feel that they are in a place of learning, not in a community or social center. In a system that respects the individual right to choose a learning path, there needs to be a strong symbol of the value and meaning of learning, and the *fmf* school must provide that symbol.

4. HOW TEACHERS FIT INTO THIS LEGAL STRUCTURE.

The status and role of teachers has to change dramatically to achieve the level of professionalism needed in *fmf* schools. We will discuss the classroom role of teachers in Ch. 4: The Classroom Revisited; here we describe the legal and organizational characteristics.

Before doing so, we must clarify some assumed constraints: first, we assume that the number of teachers will remain in the range 2 - 4 million people, and second that the total school budget will remain roughly constant as a proportion of GDP. Since salaries and benefits make up more than half of school expenditures, average salaries are therefore constrained to remain roughly constant in inflation adjusted terms, and are assumed to remain in roughly the same position relative to other salaries in the economy. Two major consequences follow:

The large number of teachers guarantees a wide spread of skills, aptitudes, interests and circumstances;

In competing for talent with other careers, teaching will retain roughly the same level of attractiveness as it currently has.

Hence, major breakthroughs in teaching capability will have to come from changes internal to the school system, not by changes in the intake of people into the profession.

Additionally, we observe that 3 million people working in an industrial enterprise inevitably became industrial workers, expecting industrial job conditions, such as uniform contracts and wage scales. Hence, if we wish to achieve major breakthroughs in teacher effectiveness we have to change from this industrial approach and exploit the characteristics of the dynamic network enterprise, which emphasizes using to the utmost the skill and commitment of every individual worker.

As a result, an *fmf* teacher is treated as a special form of professional, working within a professional framework of training, compensation and work conditions. The numbers and variety of people in this new profession suggest that there will be differences between this profession and the more traditional professions, such as law and medicine, but many aspects will be similar.

We therefore propose the following guidelines:

I. Teachers will be required to belong to a legally established professional body, which is responsible for policing compliance with its standards;

II. This body is responsible for defining levels within the profession, and administering examinations for entry into any given level;

III. Teachers are required to renew their credentials every 5 years, and encouraged to pursue regular additions to their credentials as one accepted way to augment their salary and conditions of employment;

IV. The professional background and qualifications of all people employed by any public school are made readily available to the public and specifically to prospective students/parents;

V. Terms of Employment:

a. since students and parents require a level of stability extending over at least an academic year, teacher contracts extend for minimum periods of typically 3 years, with a renewal notice period of 6 months by either side; longer contracts can be made by mutual agreement;

b. gross violations of ethical or professional behavior by a teacher or Principal can result in immediate dismissal, with appeal to special independent arbitration boards;

c. non-renewal of contract requires 6 months notice, but no cause;

d. dismissal for poor performance or refusal to meet the terms of the contract can occur only after a period of at least 3 months written warning and clear guidance on how to reinstate acceptable performance;

e. across schools, there is no principal of uniformity of salaries, of conditions or hours of work, other than basic State mandated guidelines;

5. HOW STUDENTS FIT INTO THIS LEGAL STRUCTURE

Students' expectations and approaches to school will be shaped by a world where knowledge skills are vital, where technology inhabits every corner of their lives, where a network of family and friends provides a personal information and support network (positive and negative), and where the media is feeding them a cacophony of information. Their family cultures will span the globe, and their English language skills will vary from excellent to nonexistent. Their parents will have a great deal of information (accurate and otherwise) about learning, teaching, the brain and the "best" schools, and frequently will expect to be listened to by school personnel. They may demand traditional or progressive schools, special education services and much more; many of their demands will seem unreasonable and unsatisfiable. Today we see just a hint of this environment.

Students are clients of *fmf* Schools, and look for schools that can help them fulfill their learning goals.

Different students will refine these goals at different ages: some will remain vague throughout their school career, some will be preparing for college from an early age, some will plan for non-academic futures and many will change and evolve as they mature. Students (together with their parents) are responsible for managing their education to achieve their learning goals, and they see different schools as opportunities to further their ambitions. They look to schools to provide professional advice on how to progress through the system, particularly which certificates to prepare for as stepping stones to their ultimate certificates.

The primary message students and parents will hear from schools is, "This is what we can and cannot do to help you achieve your goals; if this is unsatisfactory, please try another school." And parental choice of school is fundamental to the *fmf* system. However, it is a choice from whatever public school services are available. Parents have little power to force a school to teach different subjects or use different methods.

It is therefore vital that each school assesses carefully the readiness and capacity of every incoming student, and signs an appropriate contract with the student/parent stating what can reasonably be accomplished in 6 - 12 months.

Students are legally required to attend a certified *fmf* school until the legal age appropriate to each State.

6. FUNDING OF FMF SCHOOLS

As in most other enterprises, "follow the money" is a sure way to understand the power structure. Bearing that in mind and following the requirement of the Social Compact, money must flow to the student/parents to empower them and ensure their overall control; the current process, in which central management funds schools, empowers central management at the expense of schools, and schools at the expense of student/parents. Changing this flow of money is both a practical and psychological imperative, supporting student/parents in their ability to transfer between schools and to be treated as paying clients.

Funding is provided by the State Department of Education in the form of an educational account for each student. Money in this account can ONLY be used to pay certified schools or institutions for qualified expenses, but student/parents never receive actual money. Parents sign (as they would when using a credit card) and the school (the equivalent of a merchant) bills the DoE, which debits the student's account. To reduce bureaucracy, student transfers between schools is typically allowed only between semesters and the number of chargeable items is kept to a minimum.

The amount of funding per student is a political decision: issues such as extra payments for disadvantaged students, special inner city allowances and any other adjustments deemed necessary for fairness are open political decisions and the results are visible for everyone to see.

Student/parents receive the equivalent of a lump sum, and decide how to use it most effectively. Some may decide to pay extra for special physical or educational facilities (where these are available), other may opt for a "mainstream" environment with special additional tuition: these decisions are best made individually for each student depending on what is available. Schools will have an incentive to provide special facilities, which attract higher payments.

This approach has the merit of visibility and direct cost control, coupled with parental choice.

LEARNING CENTERS AND COUNSELORS

The *fmf* School System has an additional structural element - the Learning Center - that exists today only weakly and informally.

fmf Learning Centers are State certified not-for-profit institutions, whose purpose is to promote better learning and learning management; they are available to all parents and schools in the surrounding community. Staffed by experts in child development and learning strategies, the Centers provide evaluation and counseling services, and in doing so channel learning research and best practices. A part of each student's funding is provided for using these services, and is expected to be used by most students.

These centers play an especially important role for parents with preschool children, providing early diagnosis of any special learning characteristics (including special gifts), and to parents who need help to navigate the *fmf* School system. Virtually all mothers know that the first months and years of their baby's life are the most critical: a time when good health and good habits have maximum impact on the baby's future growth. We have evolved a set of medical practices supporting mothers in creating a healthy physical environment for their babies and diagnosing babies' early health problems, and 'learning health" requires a similar set of services.

Education research provides insight into the various patterns of learning progress of young children, and a great deal can be done to identify a child's learning strengths and weaknesses in the critical years before grade school. We know for example that the early (e.g by first grade) diagnosis and treatment of many forms of reading disorder would alleviate many later learning failures, saving untold emotional pain and learning costs. The arguments used so persuasively to bring about national programs of early age preventive health care apply equally well to learning, and should be a part of any modern school system.

The counseling service is available throughout the student's school life, and offers periodic check-ups, guidance on treatments for special learning characteristics, and referrals to specialist help or special *fmf* Schools. It does not deal with the broader array of challenges faced by growing children, such as anorexia or drug use, but collaborates with other counseling services specializing in these conditions.

Learning Counselors have special training and degrees, and like medical professionals they have different specialties. The general Learning Counselor matches most closely an MD specializing in internal medicine, and provides the first line of case management. Other specialties will evolve, especially around common problems such as dyslexia, or around special talents. The position of Learning Counselor provides a career path for outstanding college graduates and for certain teachers who want to make a career transition. It requires serious academic study and qualifications, and experience of teaching practices: salaries should be comparable to those of medical doctors in general practice. A Counselor should be capable of understanding the latest research on learning and how to integrate it into practical advice. As we realize that "learning health" and bodily health require similar levels of research and professional knowledge, we will evolve a form of Learning Counseling based on scientific studies and theories, and move away from the current approaches to teaching, which resemble medicine at the start of the twentieth century

However the Learning Center is unlike a medical center in one very important regard; it is not solely concerned with fixing problems. Children of all learning capabilities have their own needs, including the academically brightest, and Learning Centers go to great lengths to avoid the appearance and the actuality of providing only remedial services for students with "problems". Both the Social Compact and the need to move away from a failure model of strengthening learning habits, require an attitude that each child has their own way of learning, and their progress should be measured against their own goals. Today too many students go out of their way to avoid getting help because of the stigma associated with it.

IN BRIEF

The organization of a public school system has a profound effect on how learning occurs, and we need to move from an industrial style of organization to the new model gradually being adopted by other major enterprises - a network of distributed units that puts significant responsibility near where the work is carried out. We now have the technological capability to create a state-wide or nation-wide infrastructure to support such a public school system, and allow individual schools to benefit by adapting to local conditions and by having direct access to the latest research.

The State has a key role to play in setting the rules, licensing, auditing and supplying the infrastructure to individual schools, but it does not operate schools (except in emergencies). The State also determines the new 3R's part of the curriculum (see Chapter 4: The Classroom Redefined).

Perhaps the most significant shift is that *fmf* schools provide a value-added service: specifically the ability to help a student progress from their present academic state to a new level, as agreed in an up-front contract. The schools are responsible for the services spelled out in this contract, but not the overall educational success of any student.

Schools are not-for-profit organizations, with a Principal and a Board, and may offer general services, such as a full elementary level curriculum, or a specialized service such as multiple language courses. Teachers are professionals with individual contracts with their school, and belong to a professional organization that enforces the standards of the profession.

The funding is organized as an educational account for each student, which can only be used at an accredited institution, via a special "credit card". The control of where and how this money is spent lies with the student/parent, within rules specified by the State.

A new component in the *fmf* school system is the Learning Center, which offers learning guidance and diagnostic services to student/parents throughput their school career.

A further description of different types of *fmf* school and possible paths through them is given in Chapter 4, in the section titled, "Types of *fmf* School."

4.
THE CLASSROOM REDEFINED

THE EDUCATIONAL PHILOSOPHY

A small number of principles guide the educational practices in *fmf* schools, and these principles are embedded in the design, so that they are naturally present as a base for all decisions, both during the initial formulation and in the subsequent evolution of the system. Here we concentrate on those generating either the most important or the most novel consequences.

We first state a meta-principle, which embodies the earlier idea of mutually reinforcing decisions. All educational goals and practices should embody the rights and responsibilities given in the Social Compact, and the organizational ideas given in Chapter 3, "The Public School System Re-organized."

Stemming from this and from the importance of the Social Compact we identify principles encapsulating the educational consequences of the Social Compact:

Principle 1. Wherever possible, educational practices should strengthen and support students in their self-management of their individual learning paths, and in their responsibility to become effective citizens.

Principle 2. The ultimate responsibility for the educational outcomes for any student lies with that student: parents have a legal responsibility, and play a very influential role, but it is secondary to the student's responsibility. This principle shapes almost everything in **fmf** *schools, from testing to homework. The system proactively encourages and supports students to assume this responsibility;*

Accepting this responsibility fully and effectively will challenge most students, and those most likely to make the best use of the system will have a strong motivation to learn; it is this motivation that enables successful students to sustain their efforts for twelve years, and as a corollary students lacking motivation are unlikely to do well and unlikely to remain in school and graduate. To offset the many competing demands on students' time and energy, *fmf* schools put near the top of the priority list the need to continuously encourage and support each student's motivation.

Principle 3. Encouraging and supporting each

student's individual motivation to learn is a key component of the *fmf* educational philosophy and is given significant resources and teacher time. Teachers become constant advocates for the benefits of learning, and become adept at teaching to the unique motivation of each student.

Principle 4. Students progress along their learning paths at their own rate and with no public comparison with other students; there is no one favored path through the system

Using these four principles, we can now describe the educational ideas and practices that give *fmf* Schools their unique characteristics.

STANDARDS

We start the description of the educational structure of the *fmf* system by describing how standards are set and students are assessed; these two features act as the steering mechanism for any school system. (The constant reference to "teaching to the test" emphasizes this fact in today's system.) Until this point readers may have wondered why the *fmf* school system does not degenerate into chaos, producing graduate students who are useless to employers, society and to themselves, so we explore this issue further before giving the specifics of the design.

Who should determine the standards or the content of the different parts of the curriculum? The historical answer has been for the key stakeholders in society to delegate the decisions to the State and the educational establishment - and then to complain that the standards are too low. The *fmf* schools' answer is more direct, and starts with the recognition that students, parents and society all have a vital stake in knowing how well prepared are graduating students, and all parties need to trust the standards and the assessment process. Employers, colleges and others must be convinced that a certificate of mastery means exactly what it says – this person has demonstrated the level of competence defined by an absolute standard, known and understood by everyone. The student needs to know that obtaining the certificate has real meaning, and is a valuable asset worth struggling for.

The natural way to establish this shared trust is to give the responsibility for defining the standards (and carrying out the assessment) to the groups having the largest stake in the integrity of the process, not to the people responsible for training the students. In particular, graduation standards should be defined and assessed by groups outside of the school system, but prior milestones are under the control of the educators.

This approach to graduation standards clearly distinguishes the definition and measurement of success from the means to achieve it, putting the responsibility where it properly belongs: the real world defines the graduation standards and carries out the measurement, while students and teachers decide how to prepare to meet them. By contrast, having the school system both prepare students and measure their success encourages floating standards and self-deception. It contributes substantially to distrust of the public school system, which is accused of lowering standards in a misguided attempt to sustain students' interest in school.

BENEFITS TO TEACHERS AND STUDENTS

Teachers, who are no longer identified with setting standards, can become an ally of the student in learning to meet the standards. This enables teachers more easily to take on a role frequently described as "expert learner" and to assist students rather than lecture them. We shall see later that the role of teachers needs to undergo a fundamental transformation, and this realignment in the relationship between teacher and student is part of that change. It is one more step towards making good teaching possible and enjoyable.

Students also benefit directly from standards created in the real world. The *fmf* schools culture constantly focuses students on the need to prepare themselves for life after school, in a world that can be very unforgiving of failure. By properly representing this real world to students, the *fmf* school system of graduation standards encourages them to see education as the opportunity to prepare for that world, not as a way to gain a badge that they deserve simply by showing up at school. This becomes particularly significant as graduation approaches and students realize that they are working to satisfy themselves and the real world, not their teachers or the school system.

Defining graduation standards externally to the school system contributes another strand to the philosophy of *fmf* Schools. In this new view, schools facilitate a relationship that is primarily between the student/parent and the real world. Today the relationship is primarily between the student/parent and the school acting as a surrogate for the real world. There is a world of difference.

DEFINING STANDARDS FOR A COMPLEX NEW WORLD

In defining standards, philosophy and practicality go hand in hand, since it is no longer possible for schools to act as effective surrogates for the real world. Modern society needs graduates with different levels of mastery of a huge diversity of knowledge, and any attempt to reduce this diversity to one standard, such as a general high school certificate is counterproductive and likely to produce a worthless piece of paper. Only the people working in or close to a particular field have a realistic chance of understanding the important requirements for knowledge in that field or occupation; only they can realistically track the changing trends and priorities, and through their choice of standards guide the student to spend their learning time wisely. Teachers and other members of the school establishment have their own world of learning and employment, and are poorly placed to understand and represent the new world in all of its complexity.

This difficulty has always been recognized for the transition from school to college, where the high school certificate plays a minor role and colleges set their own standards. College bound students often take a test designed by an external organization, such as the SAT or the ACT (about 2 million students a year between them), and we accept the implication that a high school certificate alone has little to say about a student's readiness for a four year college.

In its early years, the high school certificate was a proud badge of readiness to participate in American industrial life, but it has outlived its usefulness in our post-industrial society. As a natural consequence of having the school system define graduation standards, we have come to regard the school graduation certificate as a badge of past achievement, and only indirectly as an assertion of competence to do something. We reinforce this attitude by phrasing some standards requirements in terms of time spent, such as requiring three years of mathematics. We imply a level of student competence, but in reality we achieve whatever the school system defines and assesses; an often unsatisfactory blend of good intentions and modest achievement.

STANDARDS AND EQUAL OPPORTUNITY

True educational opportunity requires that all serious students can demonstrate their ability to succeed, whether or not their future is academic. In practice, the current system divides students into those who apply to selective colleges and the rest. The first set is offered a clear view of the necessary achievements and multiple ways to demonstrate them, the "rest" are offered a high school certificate of widely varying quality. As this badge of school success loses its value, students/parents look for a replacement, and are settling on the college degree as the new badge of entry to the good life, with the consequence that everyone will ultimately want to go to college.

Unless we significantly change the nature of our colleges, this makes little sense either for our students or for the nation. Offering every student the *opportunity* to go to college does not mean that every student should try to get a college education, assuming that we continue to mean a relatively academic education. We need to learn from the history of high schools. When gaining a high school certificate was a relatively rare achievement it had a real value especially for those students intending to go immediately into the workforce. In our commendable drive to give every child a sound education we adjusted the public school system until about seventy percent of students regularly graduate – achieved by a combination of improving schools and by adjusting standards. The result was to turn the high school certificate from a valuable asset to a basic requirement of little value, except its negative value to those who don't achieve it.

If it maintains a single monolithic standard, a public educational system in a democratic society will naturally tend towards this state, because the public will demand that the majority of students reach that standard. We can choose to repeat this process at the college level or we can correct it in schools and preserve colleges as specific institutions that are valuable to some members of society, but not a requirement on the path to reasonable success.

At some point we have to recognize and build into our educational system that there can be many paths to success and prestige, and academic colleges are just one of them. One vital step is to create multiple high quality certificates, valued by students and society and reflecting knowledge skills of real value. Only the marketplace can do this with the requisite accuracy, flexibility and conviction. That marketplace includes academic colleges, vocational colleges and an increasing diversity of post-secondary educational offerings, such as distance learning, together with groups representing different employers. Ultimately only the student can choose between these alternative paths to personal success. The result can be fair provided the alternatives offered are competitive and fairly supported, not unreasonably biased towards one form of success.

STANDARDS, CAREERS AND MOTIVATING STUDENTS

The power of standards to affect behavior presents an opportunity to achieve other national goals, such as encouraging more students to become scientists. Taking a leaf from sports, *fmf* schools encourage students to identify with actual scientists or lawyers or business people, for example, not only through early contact during school years, but in how standards are presented. Each appropriate group in society presents their case for students' attention through the ownership and promotion of their standards. Scientists show the magic in uncovering the mysteries of nature, industry advertises the impact of a successful business, governments show the possibilities of public service, and all of them simultaneously make clear the need for students to clear certain educational hurdles – specific hurdles defined by those interest groups, reflecting the realities of pursuing such a career. The power of the approach comes from the passion and commitment of the engaged adults appealing directly to students, without needing the schools as intermediaries, and, in demanding high standards, the adults enhance their own standing in the eyes of the students.

When *fmf* school students hear actual scientists saying, "If you want to join us, this is what you need to achieve," they hear a far more powerful invitation than any offered by the school system. As a result, students approach an *fmf* school graduation assessment much as they would a try out for the school play or sports team – it is an opportunity to be accepted into a desirable group – and, if unsuccessful the first time, they can try again later. Nerves and fear come with any serious test, but facing a test that offers the entrance to a desirable career is very different from facing one that simply labels you.

All *fmf* school students, not just the college bound, are constantly encouraged to think realistically about their future, and the schools constantly reinforce the message that education is the key to achieving the freedom to choose a future career. Young children may not be ready to think specifically about a career, but they can be encouraged to see education as giving them the freedom to choose their future. We seem to have lost the ability, once considered a vital part of schooling, to position education as the great opportunity for every child. We have allowed our children to confuse going to school with getting a good education – showing up is not 80% of school success.

STANDARDS BOARDS

We can formalize these ideas by creating a series of Standards Boards, which function similarly to current standards boards, but with some important differences.

Society has a vital interest in guiding students to learn appropriate forms of knowledge, and students need to know what society expects of them, so published standards are necessary, and these need to be professionally designed, stable and meaningful. Some of those standards represent knowledge that society expects students to master as part of their commitment in the Social Compact to become effective citizens. Some other standards represent knowledge required by important elements of society as a prerequisite for entry into their institutions: colleges and professional groups have an interest in these standards. Other interest groups can create a Board and issue standards covering topics that they believe some students will want to include in their elective courses. The standards of one Board may incorporate those of another Board, adding only those topics that are specific to their needs. In particular, many standards would include the State mandated 3R's Standard, as a requirement.

Given the need for public trust, each Standards Board is certified by the federal government except the 3R's Standard Board which is appointed by each State. Support and management of an elective Standards Board come from its members; the government does not determine these standards or play a direct role in their development. However, bodies such as the National Academies, the National Science Foundation, the National Institute of Health and the National Endowment for the Arts would naturally play a role in their relevant Board, lending their expertise, credibility and understanding of the national interest. Industry plays an equally important role, being represented by major manufacturing and technical organizations. Since setting standards requires professional expertise, which is available today in the education establishment, in academia and in some commercial organizations, the actual process of drafting the standards would be carried out by experts, including those who understand child development.

A common form of organization of an *fmf* Standards Board is the non-profit membership organization, comprising the members, the Directors and a staff that carries out the professional work. The members are the representatives of various interest groups or stakeholders with direct concerns, and members have obligations and/ or dues that dissuade casual participation. Ultimately the Directors, representing the members, have the final responsibility for the choice of standards, which may be developed in house or, more often, through a contract with an expert organization.

The Board that sets the standards is also responsible for operating the assessments process, typically via a contract with an organization with the necessary technical and operational experience. When taking a graduation test with a particular Standards Board, students pay a fee, which is regulated by the government, and the appropriate amount is included in the educational dollars given to each student. The fees cover the major operational costs of the standards Board, but the administrative and staff costs are born by the members through membership dues.

PUBLIC CONFIDENCE IN STANDARDS

Given the importance of these graduation standards and assessments, the process for developing and managing them needs to be very transparent, and open to public analysis and critique. For example, each Standards Board publishes how any specific tests are designed, scored and scaled, and the nature of the guidelines given to all examiners. Current testing practices are based on decades of experience with multiple choice tests, but the broader assessments required for *fmf* school graduation require ongoing research to refine them and eliminate actual or perceived bias. As a research based system, *fmf* schools and Standards Boards expect informed criticism and debate, but this full openness does not imply democratic or political decision making. The Directors of each Standards Board make the key decisions, and are responsible for the results. The current quasi-democratic decision making of State standards and tests frequently leads to political decisions, especially where cultural sensibilities are involved. *fmf* schools attempt to take proper account of such sensibilities by having all the information and comment made public, but ultimately each Standards Board is required to act in the interests of the members. The only Boards that are subject to political guidance are the States' 3R's Standards Boards and the

Federal Civics Standards Board, discussed later.

DEALING WITH POLITICALLY CONTENTIOUS ISSUES

How does the *fmf* Standards process deal with a contentious issue, such as Intelligent Design? Proponents could propose it to a State Board as part of the 3R's Standard, but that is an unlikely route, given the heavy emphasis on limiting that specific curriculum to accepted core requirements. Another possibility is to submit it to a scientific Standards Board, for example the Board dealing with evolution. If the scientific community decides that Intelligent Design is not a scientific theory, and is not properly part of any science standard, the advocates of Intelligent Design can pursue the issue by continually trying to convince the scientific community and their Standards Board, or they can attempt to have it incorporated into a different standard. If this different standard incorporates Intelligent Design, a number of students are likely to study the idea, but not as science.

Such an outcome would imply that there exists in society a significant body of people who both believe in Intelligent Design and regard understanding it as a prerequisite for joining them or working with them. Such a group is defining a curriculum for one of the elective courses in the *fmf* School system, and face the problem of all curriculum designers – what to leave out from an overcrowded curriculum. They are motivated to include only those elements with high value to their members. Today it is sufficient to believe abstractly that students "ought" to learn such an idea, and to lobby to have it included in the basic curriculum, without being responsible for the practical demands on student time. The *fmf* standards approach is self-correcting, in that some significant group in society has to accept that a proposal, such as Intelligent Design, is a requirement for their particular needs, and enough students have to be willing to spend their valuable educational dollars to learn about it.

THE NEW 3R'S STANDARDS BOARD

The New 3R's part of the curriculum is explained in the section entitled Curriculum, later in this chapter, but how the standards are defined and the students are assessed is covered here.

This part of the curriculum represents a vital interest of the State, namely that each adult should be able to act at least minimally as a citizen, and therefore it is appropriate that the Standards Board should be set up and run by the State. This Board should adhere to the same principles of openness and transparency as every other Standards Board, but the Board Members are appointed by the State.

THE NEW CIVICS STANDARDS BOARD

The New Civics part of the curriculum is explained in the section entitled "Curriculum", later in this chapter, but how the standards are defined and the students are assessed is covered here.

There will be a newly created New Civics Standards Board that manages the standards and assessments for the *fmf* New Civics curriculum, and this body must represent a vital interest of the Federal and State governments - the education of citizens who are aware of and competent to perform their new and more complex civic duties. It is therefore a political arrangement requiring a political solution.

Given the low esteem currently enjoyed by most politicians, a cynic might doubt whether such a body can be formed, but an optimist can see *fmf* schools as an opportunity to rebuild a belief in our political institutions and in public service. A key challenge is to find the right balance between representing the real debates about our society, and in insulating the Civics Standards Board from daily politicking. *fmf* schools take as a model the Supreme Court. The Civics Standards Board is independent of the Federal Administration, and its Directors hold their positions for life. Given the potential importance of the Board's decisions and the properly political nature of the role, each Director is appointed by the Administration and approved by the Senate.

The Board operates according to a special Charter and generates a part of the Mandatory curriculum, and it has several major responsibilities, in keeping with the common philosophy and structure of *fmf* schools' Boards. Two in particular require special attention: the organizing of assessments and the certification of Civics teachers.

How do we decide whether a student is a competent citizen? Some parts of the answer mirror those in any academic subject. For example, does the student understand enough of America's history, the Constitution and the workings of the Federal and State governments? Other parts are more practical. Does the student know how to vote nationally and locally, how to contact their State or US Congressman, and perhaps as importantly have they actually experienced these actions in a way that diminishes fear or indifference in participating in democracy. At the deepest level, do students know how to make the democratic process work for them, and for others? Wealthy educated people have enormous advantages in making even a truly democratic process work for them, but political fairness and stability require all people to be able to make their views felt and seek redress for their grievances, and not only by voting in a Presidential election. One of the central responsibilities of the Civics Standards Board is to promote the importance of being an effective user of our democratic processes, and to set up meaningful courses and assessments to persuade students to take civics seriously. As with other subjects, a few multiple choice tests cannot hope to achieve the necessary level of seriousness, and *fmf* school students are confronted with serious milestone assessments in Civics, all managed by the Civics Standards Board.

Selecting and training teachers for the New Civics Curriculum poses special challenges, since teaching Civics in *fmf* Schools raises issues not generally found in the current school system and it requires sensitivity to some specific issues. For example, it is a compulsory course, in potential violation of the core value espoused by *fmf* Schools – the right and the responsibility of students to manage their own education. Teachers who lean too heavily on the legal requirement of students to attend the courses will either fail or will undermine the culture of self-reliance promoted in other courses. On the other hand, teachers who fail to promote the seriousness of becoming an effective citizen can do untold long term harm, and are not supporting the Social Compact, which requires students to learn how to become effective citizens. Additionally, the independence of each *fmf* school potentially allows teachers to deviate from the carefully defined framework of the curriculum, and espouse personal views or teach in an unacceptably biased way. For these and other reasons, the role of the Civics Standards Board in certifying Civics teachers takes on a special significance.

Ideally, the Civics Standards Board uses its power and prestige to attract and train a cadre of teachers who specialize in Civics and who believe in its importance. It provides special training courses for potential Civics teachers, and requires practicing teachers to be re-certified by the Board every 5 years. The training focuses on the special responsibilities, attitudes and methods required to successfully represent the Board's standards and limits. The Board also runs a special Review Panel for accusations that a teacher has seriously violated the code of ethics required of a Civics teacher.

Although the Civics Standards Board is constructed according to the same principles as other *fmf* Schools' standards bodies, it plays a very special role in our education system. Through this institution American society expresses its ideals and its conviction that students should understand those ideals and know how to make our institutions work to support them. Society gives the Board the prestige and the resources to be effective and makes it one of the major educational institutions in the US, responsible for educating and assessing all students in Civics and for giving specialized training and certification to about a fifth of all teachers. The Board brings clarity to an often muddled discussion about the meaning of "public" in public schools. It makes clear (a part of) what we require schools to do in the public interest, and recognizes that this particular public interest is different from the desire to have more computer scientists or linguists. The prestige and commitment of the Board rescues Civics from being the stepchild of the curriculum, and reaffirms our faith in public service. It is one of the most important parts of *fmf* Schools.

Each State has a legitimate right to have a part of the New Civics Curriculum be specific to their State, and a provision is made for each State to add this to the main Civics Standard.

DEFINING STANDARDS FOR THE LIBERAL ARTS CURRICULUM

One challenge for *fmf* schools is to find an interpretation of the fundamental liberal arts idea that is consistent with the Social Compact and the characteristics of our new world.

Breaking the problem into two parts suggests much of the answer; deciding who defines the standard and who enforces it. Who enforces it is easily answered; any body that chooses to require it as an entrance requirement. In this way, society expresses its belief in the value of the liberal arts education, in several different senses: whether the content forms a valuable core of knowledge for various roles in society, whether *fmf* schools can prepare students to master the knowledge, and whether the demand on the students' time is worthwhile. Different parts of society can legitimately answer these three questions differently, and can change their answers over time. A successful outcome results from the interaction between the definition of the standard, the effectiveness of the students' learning and the balance of the value of this education compared to more specialization. The *fmf* schools mechanism allows each part of society, including the students, to vote, and to live with the consequences. It is too easy today to vote for a broad liberal arts education, without weighing either its real appeal to society or the opportunity cost of missing other forms of education.

Two practical solutions are likely to evolve: one has a distinct Standards Board for Liberal Arts, the other incorporates elements of a classical Liberal Arts curriculum in another standard. If a Liberal Arts Standards Board does a good job of creating a flexible and useful standard, it is likely to be used by other Standards Bodies who have little incentive to expend resources on creating their own. However, some institutions may require a unique flavor of the curriculum, and would be motivated to augment the common standard. In particular, Liberal Arts Colleges are likely to have specific entrance requirements that exceed a general education in Liberal Arts.

STANDARDS FOR EMPLOYMENT

Many students graduate and go directly into employment, and they too need to know the standards required by different employers.

fmf schools use the same approach to different forms of employment. It should be the responsibility of employers' groups to define the minimum standards of entry to their types of employment. That is not to say that they are legally obliged to deny work to someone without the qualification, nor accept someone with it, but it gives a realistic indication of the minimum requirements expected. It is probable that a very few standards would be sufficient for most forms of general employment, backed up by specialist standards for subspecialties, such as catering, and cost pressures will drive employers in this direction. Since the *fmf* schools curriculum has a Core requirement, many external standards will take the form of requiring a certificate of mastery of the Core, plus specific additional standards defined by the external group. However, the Core covers far less than the current "mile wide and an inch deep" curriculum today, but sets meaningful standards for the included topics. An employer can rely on a Core Certificate of Mastery to mean specific knowledge capabilities and skills. It is not a measure of the hours spent in a classroom.

INTERNAL SCHOOL STANDARDS

With these graduation level standards in place, the educator community can define intermediate standards at meaningful pre-graduation levels, suitable for deciding whether students are ready to study at a next level within the school system. It is not intended that these intermediate "milestone" standards provide annual tests; they are intended as meaningful stages of learning in any given subject, and as checkpoints for student/parents (and teachers) to assess whether sufficient progress has been made to reach the intended destination. Since they are designed to assess whether a student is ready to take courses at the next level within the school system, it is appropriate that these standards are defined by the school system.

It should be noted that there are no high stakes annual tests in the *fmf* system, and any measures of school effectiveness are separated from the assessments of students against curriculum standards.

CERTIFICATES

Though a school system has the broader mission to offer students a rounded education, the primary focus of most students, parents and commentators is the ability of students to satisfy the graduation standards erected by society, and this requires some sort of "badge": typically a piece of paper attesting that the holder has attained the requisite level. In the *fmf* system this role is played by the Certificate.

For every major standard there is a Certificate (possibly several at different levels), awarded by the appropriate Standards Board to passing students, and the implication is that to participate in the activities represented by that Board (e.g. going to college) students must possess the appropriate certificate(s).

Traditionally these certificates would be regarded as exit badges, signifying completion of certain courses, and thereby focusing attention on the school, and school attendance, which leads quickly to a focus on habits, school practices and stereotypical learning paths. By contrast, *fmf* graduation certificates attempt to capture the results achieved, which is a more relevant criterion and has the additional benefit of allowing more flexibility in how the results are achieved. What matters is whether students have the competence required by the standard, not how they acquired that competence. Certificate assessments potentially cover all the material prior to that point. They are specifically designed to eliminate the idea that a student can learn something for the test and then forget it. Knowledge is assumed to be cumulative, with each level requiring and building on the prior level.

It is also worth noting that there is no attempt to describe comprehensively a student's overall "educational level", and there is no general requirement to attend a given number of courses for specific amounts of time (except possibly for parts of the mandatory State component of the curriculum). Said differently, in the *fmf* approach the States create standards for the subset of school learning that can reasonably be standardized and tested, and for which society has a meaningful interest (as expressed by the creation of a 3R's Standards Board), but it does not attempt to formulate standards that encompass all of students' school learning, nor compel students to spend the large majority of their time on subjects mandated by society.

ASSESSMENT

The focus of assessment in the *fmf* system is to allow the student to demonstrate the appropriate level of knowledge and understanding. It is essentially a pass/fail system, with as much feedback as possible given to the student. A student may sit the exam as often as required, and will be offered the opportunity to learn from the detailed feedback on areas of knowledge or skill that are lacking.

Assessments are not viewed as obstacles to challenge the students, nor ways to sort students. They are described as the opportunity for the student to demonstrate a level of capability, and are conducted in that spirit, not as traps designed to ferret out deficiencies. As a result they are adapted to individual student's needs and include concrete elements to reduce nervousness and failure due to environmental concerns. They are not competitive, nor do they rank students.

None of this implies that the assessments are easy to pass: some may be extremely hard and suitable for only a small proportion of students. However, unless explicitly included in the standard (and rarely so), assessments are not considered to be a general test of fitness to survive mental or physical challenges. They do not include an implied element of fitness, such as the ability to overcome nervousness on the day.

Graduation level assessments are the most significant and are designed to assess whether the student meets the stated criteria, which may differ in style from one standard to another. For example, the mastery of a large number of facts may be very important for one standard, but, for another, the emphasis may be on the ability to think through an original problem. At this level the assessment will certainly include material that was learned years earlier: it is not an "exit exam" designed to test the recent year's knowledge. Therefore a student cannot hope to pass it solely by a last minute effort.

While graduation level assessments are carried out by the Standards Bodies, assessments of earlier stages of learning are carried out within the school system, and have the specific purpose of deciding whether the student is ready to move on to the next stage of that topic. The timing of such a test is under the joint control of the student and the school, and age is not a significant requirement. As with graduation tests, these interim tests are pass/fail and conducted with maximum feedback to the student.

The single most important point about assessment, especially when carried out at the school graduation level, is that it is convincing to everyone with a stake in the outcome: particularly the students and the organizations that rely upon them for hiring or college admission. However assessing a student's capabilities is almost as difficult a task as teaching and requires a considerable level of skill and resource. Therefore an important commitment of the *fmf* school system is to allocate a sufficient percentage of the total education budget to ensure that assessment results are convincing to all concerned.

With the current level of expertise in carrying out assessments, highly computerized multiple choice tests will play a relatively small part in a major assessment. For example, a graduation level test would probably take a week of the student's time, and consist of oral tests, computer tests and maybe hands-on tests. Practical consideration will probably dictate that a student demonstrate a sufficient likelihood of passing a graduation test before being accepted to sit a full week's assessment.

The Standards organizations carrying out the assessments will typically hire teachers, and train them to carry out the forms of assessment defined by the particular Standards Board. These teachers will normally expect to carry out assessments only for a few weeks during any year, and will take leave from their schools for a week at a time, as needed and planned in advance. Some assessments will occur during normal school vacations, but they also occur throughout the year. Teachers never test students from their own school and safeguards are built in to detect and deter bias. Over time carrying out demanding assessments becomes an alternative career path for some teachers, while others alternate between teaching and testing. Being involved in the testing process allows teachers to keep intimately abreast of evolving standards and the thinking of the Board creating the standards, and as a result they have a window into the world awaiting the students. *fmf* schools benefit from having teachers who understand the important milestone assessments, and welcome the opportunity to release teachers for the few weeks required.

THE CURRICULUM

MANY PATHS TO SUCCESS

Two radical shifts of thinking guide the *fmf* Schools curriculum. The first (discussed above) asserts that the graduation standards for the curriculum should be set by groups external to the school system – groups that have a serious interest in the competence of high school graduates. The second asserts that students choose how to allocate at least half of their school time to different parts of the curriculum.

The need for students to control at least half of their school time flows naturally from the Social Compact. Although both society and students have a valid stake in the curriculum, students can only maintain control over their education if they decide how to allocate the majority of their time. Society's claim must take lower priority.

The requirement to balance the needs of society with the needs of students strongly influences the main structure of the *fmf* Schools curriculum, which has two parts: one representing society's needs and the other representing students' needs.

THE FMF CURRICULUM AND SOCETY'S NEEDS

Any publicly funded school system must satisfy the basic educational needs of society, and history suggests that two such needs predominate: the need to prepare students for the practical challenges of living in society, and the need to train students to be good citizens. Over time the specific interpretation of these needs and the balance between them has changed, and a future school system inevitably has a different interpretation and balance from an industrial school system.

The response of schools to society's practical need has traditionally been the 3R's curriculum, and *fmf* Schools have a *New 3R's Curriculum* updating the traditional 3R's curriculum to modern needs. Its fundamental purpose is to prepare students with the *minimally required skills* to be effective in modern American society; specifically, to get a job and to handle the increasingly knowledge based demands of daily life, such as banking, traveling and buying a house.

With little effort, we could fill a twelve year 3R's curriculum with plausibly needed skills for modern life, but common sense and a commitment to the Social Compact require a better balance with other demands on students' time, and hence the emphasis on *minimally required skills*. An example of how to interpret minimal occurs in math. Virtually all adults need a firm grasp of percentages to negotiate fair credit terms, for example, but only a minority needs to understand algebra; knowledge of percentages is *minimally* required, but knowledge of algebra needs to compete with thousands of other pieces of knowledge for a space in the personal curriculum of any particular student. General assertions that every child needs "advanced math skills" are false and known to be so by students and parents alike. The frequent claims of "national importance" for advanced technical skills would be far more credible if they distinguished skills that are vital to a small but significant percentage of students from vital basic skills.

Society's second need - for schools to train students to be good citizens - takes on a particular significance as we evolve to a new world, where many social assumptions are blown away, and society needs to emphasize those skills that continue to anchor our specifically American way of life. In particular, as we move away from identifying ourselves with large groups and towards more individual self-expression, students need to understand how to balance their individual needs with the larger needs of a cohesive society. The *fmf* schools' response to this need is the *New Civics Curriculum*, which has to play a more significant role in student life than today's civics instruction, which did not merit inclusion in the "No Child Left Behind" Act.

THE NEW MANDATORY CURRICULUM

The New 3R's Curriculum and the New Civics Curriculum are both mandatory, and have prior claim on students' time over the elective courses. However the content is chosen so that the majority of students can complete the requirements by the age of sixteen using half of their school lesson time. Those students who continue at school until age eighteen will normally then be studying only elective courses, and so their average school career time spent on elective courses will reach sixty percent.

From the students' perspective, the requirement is to pass a series of milestone examinations, not to take courses for a specific number of semesters. Advanced students can avoid certain 3R's Courses by taking more difficult elective courses and passing the appropriate examinations. Their total elective course time can exceed sixty percent.

As a result, on average, *fmf* schools allocate two days per week to the New 3R's Curriculum and a half day per week to the New Civics Curriculum, with the intention that the majority of students can complete the work in ten years.

Although this is the average allocation of time over the twelve years of schooling, the pattern typically changes as the student progresses from elementary level to high school level courses. The majority of students in the early years need the same base of knowledge for all future learning paths and allocate most of their first two years to the New 3R's curriculum. The school week during these early years typically has four days devoted to the New 3R's Curriculum, one half day on the New Civics Curriculum, and another half day of sports or music or other elective. When they are old enough and have enough knowledge they start to introduce more elective courses and by the middle years of high school they typically will have completed all of their mandatory lessons and passed the appropriate graduation level of the New 3R's and Civics Curriculums. Their time and focus by age fourteen or fifteen will be on those courses that enable them to obtain the certificates of entry into the real world, not on passing milestone or exit exams of the school system.

It should be clear from the basic principles of *fmf* schools that all schools should endeavor to adapt this basic outline to each child's needs, allowing more advanced students to get through the basic curriculum more quickly, and slowing down for those students who need more time, instead of rushing them through material, which they half understand and fails them at a later stage. In a world of lifelong learning, it is better for a student to have the confidence of having mastered a useful part of the curriculum, than it is to have stumbled through a larger curriculum. Since *fmf* students do not belong to age cohorts, social groups and studying groups are different, and there is far less stigma to studying more slowly.

THE NEW ELECTIVE CURRICULUM

Balancing the mandatory curricula is the New Elective Curriculum, which encompasses practical vocational courses, specialized academic courses, arts courses and broad general courses, including sports. The selection is not based on any one theory of the best education for all children, but emerges from the interplay of student/parent wishes, the available skills and resources of the community and the contemporary needs of society. A vital task of the Federal or State Department of Education is to foster an appropriate balance between these elements, to ensure that all students have fair and informed access to the capabilities of the *fmf* Schools system, and that suitable *fmf* schools are available.

The intention is that each student can select a range of courses that go beyond the basic skills to fulfill each individual learning goal or career ambition. No one set of courses is favored by the *fmf* school system, but individual *fmf* schools may specialize in a few subjects, and the pattern of courses available in any community responds to the demand in that particular community.

In the sense of the knowledge and skills students are expected to learn, there is no Elective Curriculum: there is no one coherent body of knowledge that all students should master and which defines the ideal school education. We have argued earlier, and more fully in Appendix 2, that this ideal curriculum is impossible to usefully define, would be impossible to teach effectively and attempting to use it does more harm than good. The *fmf* school system replaces this rigid view by a dynamic set of externally defined standards, each of which implies a curriculum for those schools that offer to assist the student in meeting that standard. If we implemented this approach today, many of these external standards would be supported by some part of the curriculum found in current academically excellent schools.

However, there is far too much to learn to meet the demands of the ideal curriculum, and skimming the surface or stumbling through it under duress does more harm than good. The *fmf* approach is to challenge students to select those parts of the total possible (elective) curriculum that they find most useful or most appealing, and to motivate them to really master those parts. The fact that students make the choice and accept responsibility is a key enabler of their motivation and commitment.

While the New Elective Curriculum is designed to foster mastery of the appropriate knowledge, we need to add one further component to the strategy of developing general intellectual skills. If most people need to learn new intellectual skills throughout their lives, schools should train students how to become expert learners. Students should "learn how to learn". In explaining the *fmf* approach, we will be forced to deal with some currently contentious issues, such as learning facts versus understanding big ideas.

LEARNING HOW TO LEARN

A fortunate few high school graduates have clear ideas of how they learn, but most students have given little thought to the concept. Schools often treat learning like walking – everyone has a natural level of ability - some more than others – and with a little practice it becomes automatic. In many ways this assumption is born out by reality. When faced with the need to learn on the job, many adults do approach it automatically, having little idea of their own learning strengths and weaknesses.

Thus all the talk of us becoming lifelong learners faces the reality that most of us have little idea *how* to learn effectively, especially when there is no teacher to guide us. *fmf* schools seek to change this outcome, by making learning to learn a key goal of the curriculum, and a key strategy for dealing with an uncertain future. This new emphasis is a critical part of the shift of responsibility to the student: we recognize that students will need not only a better motivation to learn, but also new tools to help them learn in a more independent way.

HOW PEOPLE LEARN

Current school curricula have a long and traditional history, but little in the way of scientific data to assess their effectiveness or direct their evolution. Both those defects are beginning to be addressed, and, in trying to update traditional methods, *fmf* schools base their curriculum and teaching philosophy partly on the three principles laid out in "How People Learn" (National Academy Press, Washington, D.C. 1999).

In 1999 the National Research Council (one of the four National Academies) published the results of its 2-year study gathering together the latest research on "How People Learn". History may well cite this report as the beginning of a new era, in which our schools began to base their ideas and practices on the best research into the brain and the mind. Since its publication, further research and additional reports have expanded its recommendations and translated them into more direct guidance for teachers (see for example, "How Students Learn: History, Mathematics and Science in the Classroom", The National Academies Press, Washington D.C., 2005). The careful thoughtful prose of the original report offers a welcome break from the emotional rhetoric that characterizes so much of the discussion about schools, though the authors would be the first to admit that they have only made tentative steps towards a scientific approach to learning.

The report highlights three findings, chosen because they have a strong basis in research and strong implications for teaching:

Students come to the classroom with preconceptions about how the world works. If their initial understanding is not engaged, they may fail to grasp the new concepts and information that are taught, or they may learn them for purposes of a test but revert to their preconceptions outside the classroom.

To develop competence in an area of inquiry, students must:

Have a deep foundation of factual knowledge,

Understand facts and ideas in the context of a conceptual framework, and

Organize knowledge in ways that facilitate retrieval and application.

A metacognitive approach to instruction can help students learn to take control of their learning by defining learning goals and monitoring their approach in achieving them.

(Metacognitive here means that students examine how they are thinking about a problem as part of their problem solving approach.)

As a follow up to these highlights the report gives some implications for teaching, one of which relates directly to "learning to learn":

The teaching of metacognitive skills should be integrated into the curriculum in a variety of subject areas.

Namely, we cannot simply add this self-reflection as an occasional gloss for the more sophisticated students; it is an integral part of learning how to think about a subject for all students. *How People Learn* points out that each major subject has its habits and ways of thinking about the world – history being a classic example – and understanding this distinct pattern of thought is one of those intellectual skills motivating the Liberal Arts curriculum. Each time teachers rush past this depth of thinking they lose the benefit at the heart of the strategy. A similar observation applies to learning to learn; it requires the time to pause and reflect on the learning process.

Unfortunately, this rush to complete an over-full curriculum frequently stands in the way of teaching according to the three principles in *How People Learn*, and stands in the way of almost any approach deeper than skimming facts from the surface of a subject. However, students cannot simply avoid learning facts, and we have to find a way to balance the competing demands for the students' time.

THE FACTS OR CRITICAL THINKING

Referring back to "How Students Learn", the second principle states clearly that *"students must have a deep foundation of factual knowledge"*, organized within a conceptual framework. The report relates the principle to the debate about the role of facts versus ideas such as critical thinking (p7):

The essential link between the factual knowledge base and a conceptual framework can help illuminate a persistent debate in education: whether we need to emphasize "big ideas" more and facts less, or are producing graduates with a factual knowledge base that is unacceptably thin. While these concerns appear to be at odds, knowledge of facts and knowledge of important organizing ideas are mutually supportive.

The "persistent debate" in this paragraph is a polite way to describe a war that prevents real progress in our schools towards a balanced effective curriculum. The war has two primary sides, each of which proclaims a false dichotomy to rally support to their cause. The traditionalist side asserts that we must return to the habits of a (mythical) Golden Era in which all students learned a large body of factual knowledge representing basic intellectual skills and our cultural heritage. These advocates cite counter examples of bad practice, such as schools asking students to draw pictures of Einstein as part of the science curriculum, and, by implication or straight assertion, they paint progressive education and ideas such as critical thinking as woolly and wrong-headed.

Meanwhile the progressive side asserts that we now have a curriculum totally over-weighted with facts, and students leave school with little ability to think for themselves or apply the knowledge they have learned. These advocates cite examples where students spend hours learning facts by rote to pass a test, and then forget them as boring and useless. The progressives' future Golden Era will come when all students can follow their natural interests and all learning is fun.

The common thread in the reasoning is to find examples of abysmally bad teaching according to one method or the other, and then deduce that we need a dramatic swing away from that general approach. Neither side feels able to consistently argue for the balance advocated in "How People Learn".

So obvious to any neutral observer is this pattern of debate that we must ask why the debate retains its hold over so many educators, and, in doing so, we find that the arguments contain enough truth to disturb people fearful of how the system is deteriorating. We again come to one of the consequences of the industrial design of our school system - it has a natural tendency to produce many examples of both extreme behaviors feared by the warring sides. We have covered most of the arguments elsewhere, but now there is an additional wrinkle.

Teaching as envisaged in "How People Learn" is a rich,

human and complex activity, even teaching elementary math for example. It is far too complex for our level of industrialization, and inevitably becomes simplified into one of two watered down forms. One simplification of the suggested *factual knowledge base in a conceptual framework* abandons the conceptual framework, and thereby suits teachers without a full academic background in the subject, who can follow scripted lessons and use easily drilled and tested facts. This is the longstanding simplification that has been present from the beginning of our schools and is so disliked by progressive educators. It allows quantitative testing and therefore seems to provide a real education, but frequently students leave school with no conceptual frameworks to guide their future learning at college or on the job.

The other simplification has its own history, but has become more prevalent recently. It first drops many of the facts from the intended *factual knowledge base in a conceptual framework*, and then adapts the conceptual framework to fit the skills of the teacher and the student. Since conceptual frameworks in abstract have little testable meaning, the teacher and the student can, in good faith, proceed as if real learning occurs, but relieved of the inconvenience of dealing with the difficulties inherent in the intended curriculum. In its extreme form this becomes the science lesson where students draw pictures of Einstein and are tested on whether they can recognize the real picture. This is the extreme so disliked by traditional educators.

Many people understand this process and its dangers, but they draw the wrong conclusion. They see a process for teacher training and certification that is obviously broken, and they conclude that fixing it would remove most of the problems – despite decades of hearing the same diagnosis and seeing no effective remedies. The real conclusion is that we are attempting the impossible, and should redirect our energies towards developing a system that does not require three million people capable of performing at this level, but does improve our students' learning.

To do this requires us to give up preconceptions about the curriculum, and ask what sort of curriculum allows teaching according to the three principles in "How People Learn" without requiring three million teachers all to be heroic. The *fmf* solution is to accept a fundamental shift in responsibilities and control, and to couple it with encouraging students to focus on the subset of possible knowledge that is appealing to them and satisfies their real world aspirations. The *fmf* New Elective Curriculum and the external Standards Boards is part of the mechanism for resolving the conundrum, while avoiding the loss of motivation and and attainment that comes with tracking solutions inherent in the current standardized approach.

Additional parts of the answer require changes in the students and in the role of the teacher in the classroom.

STUDENT, KNOW THYSELF!

Despite its foundational strengths, *How People Learn* does not address all the elements of learning to learn; we need also to include the many ways one student can differ from another and how these differences can affect learning. A short list of relevant personal characteristics includes gender, academic orientation, reading difficulties, planning skills, fine motor coordination, creativity, intellectual passivity and distractibility. *fmf* Schools attempt to take into account as many of these as possible, when creating each student's learning environment, but it is important that the student realizes and adapts to these characteristics too. Gaining this self-awareness is a major part of learning to learn.

The value of this skill is most obvious where a student has a marked learning disability, such as dyslexia. Early diagnosis of dyslexia not only promotes effective treatment, but also removes some of the fear and stigma felt by many students. In this instance, self-knowledge and the tools to manage one's behavior can mean the difference between feeling abnormal and feeling in control. Virtually all students find some parts of school unbearably hard, without necessarily knowing why, and for many this feeling sets them on a path towards self-doubt and choosing to be a mediocre student. Emphasizing that learning is a skill that can be learned and improved changes the sense of inevitability and strengthens the sense of personal responsibility and control.

Subtle characteristics can also have huge effects on the path taken by a student. For example, a hard working and focused straight-A's student may not realize that these admirable characteristics conceal a tendency to passively absorb ideas from books at the cost of personal creativity and independent thinking. When later at college this student finds it hard to generate original ideas and falls behind some other students, she has no self-awareness to help her adapt or deal with her first really negative learning experience. Early awareness of the tendency to acquire knowledge passively would have better prepared this student.

All of us have strong and weak learning habits, many of them unconscious. A common example concerns noise: some people seem to learn better while listening to music, whereas older people may have been trained to work well only in quiet surroundings. More generally, most people go through life with the attitude that "this is just the way I work", without understanding the impact of their style, or the options to change it. Personal choice based on self-knowledge is one thing, but ignorance of why and how we learn is another, and will increasingly become a liability.

Unfortunately, today any instruction on learning and work habits is liable to come with a heavy dose of moralizing. Students, especially, can be branded as "lazy", "disorganized" or "scatterbrained", with the implication that more effort would cure "the problem". Unsurprisingly, this form of instruction has little positive effect, and often the students resign themselves to being poor learners, and avoid learning as far as possible.

fmf School teachers cannot and do not take that attitude, because they are pledged to accept incoming students "as is" and to find ways to help them move forward. Therefore a first step is always to evaluate carefully the student's learning style, to check how self aware is the student and to agree how to factor that knowledge into the learning plan.

Combining the detailed subject by subject metacognition described in *How People Learn* with the cross-subject self-awareness of personal learning characteristics provides *fmf* Schools with an additional powerful tool to prepare students for an unpredictable future. Students are helped to acquire not only critical thinking about the world, but also the mastery of learning as a general and specific skill, so that they will be able to learn their way out of old skills and jobs into new ones.

PRACTICAL KNOWLEDGE AND CONCEPTUAL KNOWLEDGE

One issue that needs further discussion is the need for focus in the classroom. Any good communicator knows that a powerful act of communication requires a clear understanding of the message, of the audience, and of the context(s) participants bring to the meeting. Motivation is particularly important; the audience must have motivation to listen attentively and the speaker needs to know that motivation. However, following this advice is extremely hard in the current school setting, for several reasons, one of which stems from the use of a single curriculum for many purposes. How this comes about becomes clear from an example from life outside of school, in this case the problem of learning a foreign language as an adult.

We can imagine three different scenarios:

Going to Italy for a 2-week tour. The goal is to learn enough Italian to ask directions, order a coffee and to enjoy the sights.

Regular visits to Italy to meet family members. The goal is to be able to have a level of conversation, read newspapers, engage with Italians and increasingly, over time, to appreciate and enjoy Italian life.

A lifelong fascination with all things Italian. The goal is to learn the language sufficiently to understand and enjoy the culture, the history and the subtleties of Italian life.

Although learning Italian is needed in each scenario, most adults would adopt a radically different approach to suit each case. Time is one of the critical factors, and it operates in several ways. In scenario #1, learning would probably start only months before the trip, and would probably come from a book or evening classes. Scenarios #2 and #3 suggest an increasing time horizon and level of effort *known from the beginning*. Certainly in scenario #3 it makes sense to invest time as early as possible to study the grammar and to be able to read and write fluently and expertly. It is clear that a thorough grounding in the language will sooner or later be indispensable. No-one would expect to achieve this level with a few evening classes or in one trip, and we would expect to commit a significant effort over several years. By contrast, in scenario #2 conversation is the main focus and gaining the vocabulary and idioms of everyday Italian has priority. Some grammar is also important, but acquiring it incrementally is more natural and enjoyable and would be paced by the frequency and duration of the visits.

However, if we were to ignore the differences between these scenarios, we might argue that to learn Italian we should first learn the grammar, the regular conjugation of verbs, the irregular verbs and the pronouns, in the sort of organized sequence used in a traditional classroom. *Given enough time and enough motivation* this may well be the best approach, but in the real world neither of those conditions typically applies, and as adults we naturally adopt more realistic approaches.

WHY ARE WE SITTING IN THIS CLASSROOM?

Students only have so much time and motivation and we need to adapt their learning to fit their circumstances. Any other approach, and especially the one size fits all approach of today, will fail for many students.

The three scenarios for learning Italian apply to many learning situations, and students can be grouped as follows:

Students, who need a limited functional set of knowledge, given in as short a time as possible, and appealing to a concrete limited motivation. The new 3R's curriculum matches this scenario.

Students, who have a very functional view of their needs, but recognize that it will take time and effort to achieve the desired facility and knowledge. They are willing to trade conceptual understanding for solid working skills. The new Vocational curriculum matches this scenario.

Students, who have a long term goal to achieve significant mastery over the subject, enjoy immersing themselves in it, and require a sound conceptual understanding. They are willing and have the time to build towards long term mastery. The new Academic curriculum matches this scenario.

If we fail to recognize these three situations as different learning environments, many of the students in any class are likely to have low motivation and to suffer teaching inappropriate to their goals. But the uniform curriculum encourages just this confusion of purpose and we have very poor strategies for dealing with the consequences.

In theory, schools defer as long as possible any differentiation of teaching approach, until forced to stream students for logistical purposes. In practice each school has its own philosophy and set of constraints. Some are passionate about mixed ability classes and seem to care little for the individual motivations of students, others are eager to push advanced students forward as quickly as possible, and channel students into the appropriate stream. It is hard to find examples, other than schools that specialize in one type of student, of schools having a clear understanding of how to match the pace, style and structure of teaching to classes of students with similar aims and levels of competence.

To blame schools for this basic design flaw is to look in the wrong place. Our current system is not designed to function in this way; the curriculum and testing patterns fight against the more flexible approach and little research or practical experience exists to guide schools in being more flexible.

fmf Schools structure the curriculum around the idea that student motivation, purpose and competence play a dominant role in successful learning, and insist that teachers and students have a clear common idea of the purpose of any class, at least at the level of the three scenarios recognized above. The direct connection between thirty minutes of study and a student's career goal may not be obvious, but the repeated emphasis on where this piece of study fits into the longer term, and encouraging the student to find a connection to the real world can build a conviction that carries the student over the less obvious class sessions.

The same approach applies at all levels of schooling: *fmf* Schools try to offer parents and society at large a clearer view of the purpose of the curriculum, of a given *fmf* School or a class within an *fmf* School. As students and parents develop the habit of questioning for themselves the reasons for selecting one path over another, and recognizing that the choice is theirs, not the school's, attitudes change. Students realize that they must *be* a student – in many different ways – rather than an attendee at school.

TEACHERS AND CLASSROOMS

We have offered two different rationales for restructuring the public school system: the first was the moral imperative to give back to students as much control of their learning as possible; the second was the practical impossibility of training three million teachers to keep current with an expanding base of knowledge and teaching methods, and to become expert conveyors of that knowledge to students.

We now need to address the *fmf* solution to the second problem, and propose a new role for teachers. As we stated in the Foreword, we have a long way to go before we fully understand how to create an ideal learning environment for young students, but certain changes fit naturally within the *fmf* framework, and we describe those elements here.

The first step is to accept the impossibility of keeping the current model of teaching, which in a simplified form implies passing all knowledge through the head of the teacher on its way to the student. Once we can do that, two questions immediately arise: how does the knowledge get to the student, and what is the role of the teacher? We can answer these in outline only, but if we accept the adjustment and set off in the new direction we will learn how to make it work much more effectively.

We can see the broad outline of the answer to these questions in the evolution of many careers: skilled pilots now handle fly-by-wire planes and surgeons direct robotic arms to perform laparoscopic surgery. They have found ways to move the old skills into digital technologies that can be faster and more accurate, can provide detailed feedback and avoid many human errors. However, humans are still needed to guide the process. We must ask, what is the equivalent for teachers?

The answers lie on a spectrum, and the two ends of that spectrum are easily identifiable. At one end is the delivery of specific knowledge and knowledge skills. At this end we must make technology do the heavy lifting, because there is too much knowledge and too many different ways of learning it for any one person to master. The best human teaching skills will need to be channelled through new digital approaches that can adapt to evolving patterns of student behavior, can remember past strengths and weaknesses and incorporate the latest research in how different brains learn.

This will not be rows of children sitting at computers. We already know in principle how to build immersive environments that can simulate historical situations, remote physical locations and many other learning experiences that do not involve sitting in front of a screen. Classrooms of the future will look nothing like those of today, and may not exist as a room.

We also have to factor in the revolution in knowledge itself, as outlined in Appendix 1, because our challenge is not just to better teach existing knowledge but to help students acquire major new knowledge skills. This goes hand in hand with using the same knowledge technology to help students learn. We are simultaneously revolutionizing what students leann and how they learn.

At the other end of the spectrum we can see several vital roles that human teachers will need to play. Most obviously they will need to act as the guides to using the technological learning environment. This does not imply being technologically sophisticated. It is the difference between teaching someone to drive a car, and teaching them how cars work. It is a new interpretation of teachers as expert learners. Instead of spending years mastering an individual subject, most teachers will need to spend years mastering the art of learning, and will need to constantly update those skills every year of their careers, just as doctors do.

Equally important is their human role. Many students arrive at the classroom totally unready to learn, for a variety of reasons, many of which have little to do with their cognitive skills. And all students experience periods when emotional disturbances get in the way of learning. No computer that we can envisage can replace a sympathetic and trained person in helping students through these crises, nor in the positive direction can they replace the inspiration and motivation that a teacher can provide.

This is how *fmf* teachers would mirror the new approaches in other careers. Leverage the technology to the limit, and focus human energies and skills on the hard topics that people excel at.

An immediate reaction is often, "But a computer will never teach Shakespeare as well as an inspired teacher?" The response is in several parts. First, the assertion may be true for a limited number of teachers, but is not true today for many teachers, and *fmf* schools will concentrate on finding ways for those few experts to technologically clone themselves. Secondly, technology can offer enormous advantages that even the best unaided teacher cannot match. It can, for example, recreate in virtual environments the experience of living in Elizabethan England and talking to virtual Elizabethan English people, while supplying background interpretations of the language and thoughts that the student is experiencing, thus bringing the student closer to the experiences that led to Shakespeare's plays. Other uses of the technology connect the student to experts, to actors, to other students studying in different locations, and offer a variety of opinions beyond the possibility of any single teacher.

We can learn from this brief example (and Appendix 1) that our current set of assumptions about the role of technology in the classroom is so often limited by today's ideas, forgetting that in twenty years everything will be radically different and then radically different again in another twenty years. We should start planning our classrooms with this in mind.

There is another pitfall to avoid: the temptation to focus only on the dazzling aspects of technology and to forget the mundane but vital role in individualizing learning (see again Appendix 1). Each student has patterns of learning, and strengths and weaknesses, different levels of attainment in related fields, and as *How People Learn* observed, different world views. No teacher unaided can keep track or even notice all of these patterns, but good technology can weave this knowledge into each lesson, adapting the pace and methodology to suit the student. Importantly, this applies as much to the gifted student as to the struggling student. We should be as committed to optimizing the brilliance of one student in some field of learning as we are to compensating for some disability in another student.

So an *fmf* classroom is probably a space where a group of students, united by interest or skill or experience, come together to share the wisdom and support of an expert learner, who guides them through the possibilities offered by a sophisticated learning environment, adapted to the special needs of that topic. For example, a scientific learning environment may well be different from one devoted to literature or history.

With this view of a classroom, it becomes clear that an *fmf* school can be constructed in many different ways, so we suggest a few possibilities to stimulate the imagination.

TYPES OF SCHOOL

fmf Schools will evolve in response to local needs, but certain patterns will emerge across many communities. Almost all *fmf* Schools define themselves according to the knowledge and skills needed to successfully take the courses provided, and only accept students having the appropriate milestone certificates. This naturally creates three tiers of *fmf* Schools, roughly corresponding to current elementary, middle and high schools as defined by the academic level, but not determined by age.

In imagining different schools, it is important not to think of them as necessarily physically separated or together; the distinction between schools is legal and organizational, and different *fmf* Schools may or may not choose to occupy the same building. Given the history of building large community schools, a common pattern will be for several independent *fmf* Schools in the same community to share the same facilities, including space and custodial services.

Since most students take a very similar elementary curriculum comprised mostly of the New 3R's curriculum, students will typically attend one elementary *fmf* school until they have their first milestone certificate. As a result, the major challenge for elementary *fmf* schools is how to deal with students having a wide variety of starting backgrounds and abilities to progress. Local conditions generate different approaches, but a typical result is a single elementary *fmf* school with subdivisions to deal with major categories of special need, whether faster or slower paced. Teachers in each special subdivision typically have special credentials and can offer more expert services, but allocation of a student to a subdivision results from a negotiation between the *fmf* School and the parents. Sometimes a subdivision is a legally separate school, but this is usually unnecessary.

Many elementary *fmf* Schools pair themselves with *fmf* Schools that specialize in the next levels of the New 3R's curriculum, which at middle and high school level, occupies a smaller fraction of the time of most students, who typically take some elective courses. At these higher levels, students therefore typically attend more than one school, allocating enough time to a New 3R's middle or high school to complete the courses by age sixteen. The exact balance emerges from the interplay of the students' desires and the availability of courses.

At the high school level, *fmf* schools tend to specialize, especially in major disciplines such as Science, Languages and Liberal Arts; such schools may share the same physical facilities, but be organizationally independent. A high school student may spend one day a week completing the New 3R's curriculum at one *fmf* School, two days a week attending a Science *fmf* School, one day attending a Language *fmf* School and one day attending the Civics *fmf* School. Attendance at *fmf* Schools is available in units of half days.

The Civics curriculum is considered sufficiently important to warrant special teachers and, usually, special middle and high schools, while the elementary level of the curriculum is often handled by the same teachers as the New 3R's curriculum. Students are legally required to attend certified Civics courses one day per week until they have obtained the final certificate; typically this takes the ten years until age sixteen.

By the time students have reached sixteen years most are fully committed to a goal for the years immediately after school. Some are taking courses to acquire the certificates required by one or more colleges; these may be specialized academic requirements or a language requirement or a broad Liberal Arts certificate. Other students are already planning to work part time for their last two years, and obtain certificates based partly on their academic course and partly on their work. Employers who provide the appropriate training are reimbursed as a school.

Those students who have not obtained their New 3R's or Civics' certificate by age sixteen are required to continue at school and to devote two thirds of their time to that curriculum. It is a clear goal for students and *fmf* Schools for every student to obtain both the New 3R's certificate and the Civics certificate, and after age sixteen this overrides any guideline for students to control at least fifty percent of their time.

Some communities provide a facility for supervised self study, similar to some libraries today. These are eligible to receive the same student educational funds as a school, provided they offer the appropriate services. Students are required to sign up for sessions, to sign in and out, and parents are informed weekly of their attendance. These facilities are restricted to older students.

Sports, and physical activity beyond normal play, are considered a separate part of the curriculum and separate "*fmf* Schools" provide the training and the facilities, funded in the same manner as the academic courses. A minimum of 3 hours per week is considered mandatory, and is typically fulfilled in a youth "health club". Accredited sports schools and games are treated as part of the service of elective courses, but cannot consume more than 20% of any student's course load.

When students are young, the *fmf* school approach tilts towards teaching good habits with only small doses of self-reflection, but, in keeping with the philosophy that students increasingly take over responsibility for their own success, teachers prompt older students to review their own learning habits and to make adjustments. The teacher is the student's learning coach, while the student aims for independence from the crutch of someone else's guidance and discipline. Not all students make it, but all can benefit from trying, and many will master enough to become more effective in the world after school.

IN BRIEF

In this chapter we have outlined the educational component of the *fmf* public school system: the philosophy;

how standards are set and attainment assessed; the structure of the curriculum, and how we foresee the role of teachers and the function of the classroom. Books have been written on each of these topics and we clearly skimmed over many issues. Our purpose is to capture enough of the impact of adopting the *fmf* principles to show that a completely different way of thinking about public schooling can be integrated into a coherent system that has powerful possibilities and significant advantages over today's way of thinking.

Several shifts of viewpoint are required. Graduation level standards are set by society, and not by the educational establishment. The assessment of that standard is given sufficient time and resources to enable a convincing assessment to be carried out by the Board responsible for the standard. The curriculum has two mandatory components - a New 3R's Curriculum and a New Civics Curriculum - that are limited to consuming on average forty percent of a student's school career time. These are defined and regulated by Federal and State bodies. The remaining Elective part of the curriculum comes from the courses required to satisfy the student's choices of graduation certificates.

Teachers have a new role as expert learner, guide and personal counsellor to help the student navigate the intellectual and personal challenges inherent in twelve years of studying. Classrooms are learning environments that adapt to the personal learning characteristics of each student. The transmission of knowledge is primarily channeled through digital technologies, including immersive virtual environments.

Students are taught and gradually learn to take more responsibility for their learning decisions from their parents and from their teachers. By the time they graduate, students should have a significant grasp of their own learning characteristics, and how to continue learning throughout their lives. They are guided to what is valuable to society by the set of possible graduation certificates, and helped by schools to choose a path towards obtaining those certificates. There is no attempt to define a general ideal education or curriculum, no attempt to compare students nor any need to have social promotions. There are no age cohorts nor standard paths through the system. Each student carves out their own path, and takes responsibility for it.

5.
TECHNOLOGY, THE GREAT ENABLER

Committed teachers have long relished the opportunity to adapt their methods individually to each student, but until now it has been a utopian dream. As a society we create the systems that current technology enables, not the systems we would like. Industrial technology enabled industrial schools, which are inherently standardized to groups, not personalized to individuals.

However, for the last thirty-five years there has been an unceasing drive towards personalizing every aspect of our lives, starting with the early Personal Computers and continuing today with the ubiquitous Smart Phone. Digital technologies have taken the lead, but genomics and nanotechnologies are generating tools to enable Personalized Medicine, and we take for granted personalized entertainment and shopping.

Now it is the turn of schools, and the development of Personalized Learning. As we look at the possibilities, we begin to realize that there are two changes on the horizon, each a game changer for schools. The first is the technology to enable personalized learning, and the second is the development of a completely new knowledge technology.

The first is easier to visualize because we have examples all around us in fields other than learning, but it is worth pointing out some of the new possibilities. As we are painfully learning from the integration of our medical records, there are tremendous gains to be had from creating a personal environment for each student that goes with the student wherever and whenever learning occurs. This environment understands and utilizes detailed information about the student's learning quirks and history, and allows highly adaptive teaching strategies. It is owned by the student, and is not limited to school learning, but the relevant parts are made available to licensed teachers.

Assuming that we keep the student-teacher ratio approximately constant, individual learning means that much of the academic learning occurs as the student interacts with systems, but we need imagination to get beyond a vision of rows of students staring at computer displays. At a minimum we should be envisaging massive use of virtual environments to transport students to remote times and places, and massive use of remote presence to connect students to other students for debates and language learning, and to professors who are masters of their subjects, all carried out over three dimensional conferencing facilities. Many of the best educational ideas, such as learning through experiencing, are hampered by the limited opportunities for safe experimentation within any particular school, and by the limited number of outstanding teachers in any particular subject. We will eventually learn how to make available to all students opportunities to interact with outstanding learning environments unlimited by local restrictions. As we have noted earlier, the role of the teacher shifts to becoming the expert in using the array of tools.

Much of the value of the technology will occur out of sight, enabling the the organization of flexible school attendance, funding, tracking, assessment, scheduling and the plethora of practical challenges that attend any system of three million teachers and fifty million students. It took many of the tools of the industrial revolution to enable our current school system, and the new system will need the new tools.

However, we now need to look at the second aspect of the new technologies, which expands their impact, especially for schools. Here the origins of our current school system give little guidance. Twentieth century technology has not revolutionized either the curriculum or teaching methods, despite predictions to the contrary by inventors such as Edison. However, one novel feature of the new technologies suggests that exactly the opposite will happen shortly – new technologies will force us to replace many of our teaching ideas, and to continuously evolve the curriculum – because those technologies are transforming knowledge itself.

Knowledge lies at the heart of schooling – teaching students how to create, store, retrieve, and communicate it - and all of those knowledge skills are on the brink of major changes. This upheaval constitutes one of the biggest challenges and opportunities for *fmf* Schools, and we must try to figure out what is happening to knowledge and why, before we can suggest how future classrooms should function.

To get a better hold on how knowledge is evolving, we propose reversing the usual way of describing trends. Instead of describing new events with old language, we will describe old events with new language, giving a more modern picture that enables us see more clearly how to extrapolate to the future. Using modern language arises naturally if we think of knowledge as having its own technology, and use computer language to describe how that technology has evolved.

KNOWLEDGE AND KNOWLEDGE TECHNOLOGY

The idea of knowledge technology fits nicely with the metaphor of a "store of knowledge", that is, something that we can create, store and communicate. This store typically contains three inter-related parts: data or facts; intellectual skills and techniques; and understanding, ideas or concepts. A knowledge technology helps people to carry out the basic actions on this store of knowledge, and it fulfills the role of all technologies – augmenting a person's natural ability to achieve some goal. For example, if we think of multiplying two numbers as a knowledge task, we can see how a knowledge technology augments our natural abilities. We can multiply some numbers mentally, but most of us need help to multiply two large numbers, and for those problems we turn to our most pervasive knowledge technology, "paper and pencil". At school we learn the rules of place notation, how to record carried numbers, where to put the decimal point and how to show the answer. Using these rules, students need only know how to multiply single digit numbers in their head to use the knowledge technology to compute very large numbers – a simple example of extending a limited human capability with technology.

Knowledge technology is also vital for creating any significant intellectual work, which typically requires storing, refining and rearranging many thoughts. Having created this "piece of knowledge" the author typically communicates or stores it for public use by again using the technology, that is, by writing it down.

Until the arrival of computers, the vast majority of knowledge tasks required this one dominant knowledge technology, which we will call Writing. The term includes all the materials, tools and techniques required to put our thoughts "on paper": all the various forms of pen, pencil, paper, tools for reading and writing, copying, printing and the non-material rules that guide their use.

To use Writing a person needs to know how to encode thoughts into symbols (write), and to decode symbols into thoughts (read), which means learning a set of symbols and the rules for combining them into meaningful sentences. If we refer to the symbols and rules as the architecture of the knowledge technology, we have a modern way to describe some of the main events in the history of Writing.

A VERY SHORT HISTORY OF WRITING

About 3000 BCE, Release 1.0 of Writing appeared in several different parts of the world, including Sumeria (Southern Iraq) and the Nile valley in Egypt. Like most new technologies it was not very user friendly, requiring about ten years of study to master, including learning more than ten thousand individual symbols (pictograms). However it spawned a new technical elite, the scribes, and new training institutions, schools.

The next major Release 1.1 of Writing came about 1500 years later, with a major change to the architecture. Pictograms were replaced by symbols representing the syllables of speech, reducing the number of symbols required for useful writing from thousands to hundreds. It was followed about 1000 BCE by Release 1.2, which had a critical new step in the architecture. The new choice for the symbols of a written language matched them to the sounds, not the syllables, of spoken language. This was a breakthrough in ease-of-use, because it reduced to about forty the number of different symbols required for most languages (excluding variants such as capitals). With this advance Writing acquired its modern alphabetic form. The Greeks completed the process by adding vowels and produced an alphabet still recognizable today.

What happened next sheds light on our current situation. When technologies reach a critical level of power and user friendliness, the range of uses expands and the number of users typically explodes. For example, the arrival of the personal computer had an enormous impact on computing, changing how we think about it. To many people it now means either word processing or family photographs or recording CD's, not payroll processing on a mainframe.

Writing Release 1.2 signaled a similar turning point in knowledge. During the 500 hundred years following its introduction, the Greeks created the basis for our current knowledge and culture, including drama, formal geometry, logic, and philosophy. From that time, the (western) world shifted from having an oral culture to a written culture, and knowledge was transformed in type, in quality and quantity. This was a genuine transformation, not a slight extension.

Writing changed enormously how we create, store

and communicate knowledge, and, as a consequence, the type of knowledge we choose to create and use. To take an extreme example, Einstein could not have created the theory of relativity without Writing, and the same is probably true for most knowledge that exists today. New technologies transform the field in which they work, both in quantity and quality. We eat the food that agricultural technology produces efficiently, and we undertake very different journeys because we travel in cars and airplanes, not on horses. Similarly we create and use the knowledge suited to Writing technology; for example, knowledge which can be captured as text in a book.

KNOWLEDGE TECHNOLOGY, VERSION 2.

In the language of computers, we are now witnessing a new Version of knowledge technology, not a new Release, and like many new Versions it is disruptive, not yet ready for widespread use, and confusing to many who are trying it out. However it is also exciting, full of interesting new possibilities and beginning to reshape the landscape of knowledge.

History strongly suggests that this new version will trigger major changes in knowledge – in what we create, how we create, store and communicate it, and how we think of education. The example of the Greek explosion of knowledge suggests that we may be about to witness a complete shift in our culture, defining a new base of culture for many future generations.

However, we do not need to rely on history to predict major changes to knowledge – even a basic comparison suggests that Version 2 will be much more powerful than Version 1. In particular, it can create knowledge having different properties:

Interactive knowledge, engaging the student in a dialog not passively reading.

Three-dimensional knowledge, capturing the real world directly, not as a diagram in a textbook.

Smart knowledge, capable of adapting itself to the user.

Multimedia knowledge, using many ways to communicate.

Multi-linked segments of knowledge in addition to serial text strings.

Time varying knowledge, instead of text descriptions

of time changes.

The bulk of the knowledge captured and stored using Writing Version 1 has been passive, two dimensional, static strings of text, with the occasional diagram added. Considerable efforts has gone into making it as intelligible or enjoyable as possible, and finding ways to reduce our complex, 3 dimensional, shifting thoughts to an intelligible form on paper. We regard authors capable of achieving this difficult goal as well educated, even in comparison to a powerful speaker who writes badly.

Knowledge technology Version 2 will release many of the constraints of Version 1, stimulating a new burst of intellectual creativity, and allowing many different styles of thinking to contribute. Any one of the new features of Version 2 could generate interesting new forms of knowledge, and taken together, the possibilities are beyond any realistic prediction. Samples are beginning to appear, and we will look at one or two current uses in the classroom, but the main conclusion should not get lost in the detail. Unlike industrial technology, digital technology changes the very heart of what happens in the classroom – it can no longer be treated as an optional peripheral tool.

But Version 2 is only one force driving knowledge down unfamiliar paths – the Internet will contribute its own set of upheavals, and together they will leave almost nothing of the curriculum or teaching untouched.

WHAT WILL IT MEAN TO "KNOW"?

Judging from public comments, the large majority of parents are suspicious of moves to drop traditional mental skills and replace them with technology, but in other arenas we do exactly that. Many of us "know" the telephone number of a friend, but need to look it up in our cell phones when occasionally asked to provide it. We "know" it in the sense that it is reliably available whenever we need it, but technology makes it more convenient to dial by name than to remember the telephone number. No-one considers this a flaw or a weakness – simply a practical matter of time and energy.

However, will we feel the same when we have reliably and immediately available much of today's school curriculum? Will we regard it as a matter of convenience whether to remember the date of the Battle of Gettysburg, or a matter of laziness? When we have the most complex of calculations available at our finger tips, should we try to memorize the steps for inverting a matrix? In an era when only mental information was available whenever and wherever needed, having a good store of personal knowledge was a valid indicator of learning, but will it be so in the future?

The issue will become acute as we transition from "going online" to being always connected – living in a sea of information, models, advice, calculations, entertainment and every possible manner of digital processing. The critical transition occurs when we all assume that almost always and almost everywhere we have access in a timely manner to a large body of knowledge. Except in limited circumstances, such as in the telephone number example, access to remote knowledge is currently too unreliable to allow us the feeling of "knowing" something stored remotely, not in our heads. But this is changing rapidly and we are beginning to slip from consciously to unconsciously relying on remote knowledge.

For the moment parents are right to be concerned whether their children are learning enough of the techniques for using paper as a knowledge technology, because only paper is everywhere and always available. With paper there are no "hot spots" and lost connections to worry about, but when those deficiencies of the new technology disappear it will be vital that students are as familiar with the new technology as the old. As the always available remote knowledge increases, it will become increasing difficult to decide what to carry mentally and what to access when required.

"Bumper sticker" answers to the question of what to memorize are not helpful, nor can we continue the current overemphasis on acquiring facts. Experts know facts, but also know which of them are important and how to integrate them into a coherent picture, but experts do not accumulate a rag bag of facts. Our current approach of selecting a core set of facts to be accumulated as a demonstration of education is counter productive. Children cannot afford the luxury of learning knowledge simply because it is traditional – there is simply too much potentially useful knowledge to expect any standardized subset to work for all children and occasions. And worse, it leads students to approach knowledge in a way that inevitably breaks down when they leave school.

Instead we need to enable students to become "mini-experts" in several areas, so that they understand the process of gaining expertise - how to select and remember appropriate facts, how to formulate ideas and connections, how to assess arguments, how to use the new knowledge technology to best advantage and, above all, to understand how they are becoming expert and how to translate this ability to learn to other domains of knowledge.

Although many of the questions and answers about future knowledge are currently beyond our grasp, we know enough to see the need and the means to start on a new direction for schools. But we do have to realize how fundamentally technology is changing learning, and that, "a computer in every classroom" is a quaint way to approach it. Given that we cannot predict reliably how classrooms should function in the future, a key part of any solution is to instill into *fmf* Schools a culture of change, so that we can learn as we go and do not have to guess correctly what technology is bringing our way.

VERSION 2 KNOWLEDGE AND FMF SCHOOLS

Pioneering educators and researchers have already created thousands of ways to use early forms of Version 2 Knowledge in schools, and there are many excellent websites and books describing them. Here we want to connect key features of Version 2 Knowledge technology to strategic opportunities that support major goals of *fmf* Schools.

One goal of *fmf* Schools is to enable each student to get the maximum possible gain in learning, given their individual circumstances, especially for students with identified learning disadvantages, including sight or sound impairment, or a lack of fluent English. These students frequently find many text books or test papers hard to understand even if they know the subject material. In *fmf* Schools all materials are "intelligent" and multimedia, offering and accepting visual, audio and text forms of presentation. Intelligent reading tutors, for example, can highlight each word as it is read aloud by the student, correcting the pronunciation as required, and adapting the speed to the student's level of expertise. A body of research is being accumulated on the effectiveness of different strategies for dealing with specific impairments or learning styles, and the results of this research will one day be used for all students.

A second strategic goal is to have for each student immediate, continuous and long term diagnosis of learning patterns, especially when they lead to learning difficulties. We know that timely feedback to students can enable faster and more productive learning, and we can expect that capturing detailed learning experiences over months or years will provide important diagnostic data for teachers struggling to understand and change poor learning habits. Learning systems in *fmf* Schools will use the intelligence and interactivity of Version 2 Knowledge technology to record and analyze the student's eye movements, hesitations and fluency, misspellings and a steadily increasing list of parameters characterizing learning patterns. A trivial example would be to combine a current grammar and spell checker with analysis tools to identify patterns of weak grammar or spelling.

The textbook is an example of the rigidity of Version 1 Knowledge Technology (Writing), and the strategic opportunity provided by Version 2 to adapt teaching to each student's individual mental traits. Today the author of any book has to choose one linear sequence for presenting ideas or the story or the content in general. Although this can help the author to clarify the underlying ideas, it can put a large and often unnecessary strain on the student, who might grasp the material if presented in a different order. Many subjects can be approached from different directions, or presented with more or fewer examples or pieces of background. Version 2 books will be networks of segments allowing alternative, guided paths through the material, together with the ability to drill down to various levels of detail. Matching the presentation of material to each student's way of thinking could offer large gains in efficiency of learning compared to the one-sequence-fits-all approach today.

We know that different students have different "intelligences", to use Howard Gardner's term. Some students learn naturally with today's emphasis on linear abstract thinking, but others excel at practical problem solving, or absorbing information physically ("hands on"), or emphasizing visual input over spoken words. For some of these students the ability to see a 3 Dimensional object, such as a chemistry molecule, or to virtually dissect an animal, transforms incomprehensible words into clear ideas. For others the ability to see the effect of time passing - a movement, a flower blossoming or the patterns of people migrations - provides the necessary link to learning. Uncovering and exploiting these different forms of intelligence is one of the ways *fmf* Schools accept students as they are and maximize each student's achievement.

Since today we are starting from the situation of storing and communicating knowledge using Version 1 Knowledge technology, we tend to think of Version

2 Knowledge technology as a gloss, helping the less academic students to understand concepts. We might be more motivated to improve our classrooms if we reversed the thinking, and focused on the unnatural impediments created by the deficiencies of Version 1 Knowledge technology. The students may or may not be deficient, but the technology certainly is. Today a significant part of being a good academic student is this ability to overcome the barriers created by the Version 1 technology, but we can ill afford to lose the students who would succeed if those barriers were removed. Nor is this issue confined to the less academic students. The frontiers of knowledge are also expanding due to Version 2 Knowledge technology, and our most gifted students are faced with more demands on their school time. Every unnecessary barrier we place in front of them and every failure to provide them with the opportunity to master the new technology diminishes their opportunities.

NEW DANGERS

There are dangers for schools as well as opportunities. When a forty year old man, communicating over the network, can give himself the completely realistic appearance and voice of a teenage girl, we will look back on today's dangerous world as a haven of safety. However, reacting by trying to shut students into an electronic castle with very limited access to the outside world will be unacceptable. A more positive attitude is to see an *fmf* School as a place to learn about this new world, including its dangers, not as a place to give children a false sense of security. To provide the right balance of safety and openness, we will need not only technology to afford students safety, but a deeper understanding of children's developmental needs in this demanding new environment, another crucial area for research and thoughtful policy-making.

TECHNOLOGY OR TEXTBOOKS

Is this new technological world very farfetched and irrelevant to schools, when some do not have enough textbooks? Or is this yet another area where we cannot offer highly desirable learning opportunities, and justify the lack of them by convincing ourselves that "the old ways are still the best ways"?

Beyond this core argument that digital technologies will change knowledge itself, there are compelling general arguments why technology will be crucial to *fmf* schools.

One argument comes from the world outside of schools. It is hard to think of a major organization achieving sustained and substantial improvement in its main business without the injection of large amounts of technology. All signs point to the need to embed technology at the core of the business, even if it is not visible to the client: Wal-Mart being a classic example. Schools are very unlikely to be the one outstanding exception.

A second reason is the effect on students of technology-poor schools. Students live increasingly in a world dominated by technology, and already some feel that going to school is like going back in time. School increasingly takes on an unreal air, irrelevant to the "real" world, and by association the teaching can feel equally irrelevant. This is not to recommend technology as gimmickry, but technology as we expect to find it - in banks, airports and real life – helping us to solve our problems. Many schools, trapped inside the industrial system, can only react to technology by banning it, and finding out, as Mayor Bloomberg did in New York City, that parents have come to rely on cell phones for important practical parts of their children's lives, and banning them in schools is putting the needs of the system above the needs of students and parents. It is another example of where the culture and assumptions of the school system dictate unhelpful answers, rather than adapting gracefully to change.

A third reason is the opportunity cost of unused new techniques for learning. The challenge of creating *fmf* Schools is financially and intellectually enormous, and meeting the challenge needs the infusion and support of many new ideas. Many of those will come from outside of the school system, and will only be available to students if schools have the relevant technology required to implement the ideas. A significant mismatch between the technology in schools and outside of schools will severely limit how schools can profit from new ideas.

Only in a culture so unused to technological change is the need for technology at the core of its operations (in the classroom) seriously debated. However, throwing technology into today's classroom is counterproductive. As with the other necessary reforms, it doesn't work unless we change the system. So we are led back to the need to make difficult changes, and for that we need to see the opportunities that are within our grasp.

6.
LOOKING FORWARD

What can we learn about schools from our history, our current problems and from our growing understanding of the new world in front of us? Our national habit tends towards rehashing the problem side of the ledger, but there is another side, filled with assets and opportunities, which provides another way to think about our problems. By using those assets to create different and better schools for every student, we will also help to solve many of the problems that seem so intractable today. This book follows the more optimistic path, and we start here by recasting the story so far in terms of successes and possibilities.

We know from history that it is possible to create a school system which captures and satisfies a deep need in American society – to allow each newborn child the hope of a future shaped more by their own efforts than by the accidents of their birth. We know that we can endow our schools with a noble purpose, while asking them to solve difficult problems. Having done it once gives us confidence that, provided that we understand the needs of modern Americans, we can once again create schools where we jointly try to satisfy those needs. As before, when they succeed, our schools will enjoy widespread support.

Schools contribute to national success in many forms, including our wealth relative to other countries, the range of talents found in social life, and our ability to integrate many diverse cultures. They offer constant proof that our faith in "we, the people" is not misplaced.

The design of our current school system demonstrated the value of incorporating not only those social aspirations, but also the best commercial practices of the time, to create an effective organization. Early educators did not turn their backs on the the new ideas generating the industrial revolution, but incorporated them into their new vision of schooling, transforming the village school house into a powerful nationwide system. We too have the opportunity to revise the industrial school system bequeathed to us, and replace it with a modern networked enterprise that borrows from the best commercial practices. Our students can once again feel that going to school is to enter a modern forward looking institution, which is representative of the world they will later work in.

Research results on the brain and patterns of learning

accelerated dramatically in the last fifteen years, and we can and should expect to have a research driven school system comparable to other major national enterprises. We now have the technology to connect schools to universities, hospitals and to commercial organizations and reap the benefit of a culture open to change, while protecting students' safety. Schools can offer teachers the prestige of working at the frontier of knowledge about our most fascinating organ, our brain, and simultaneously the satisfaction of offering a vital service to our children.

When schools are operating at the leading edge of learning technology, incorporating the latest research about the mind and the brain, interacting with other research institutions, and challenging society to understand and respond to their learning needs, we will know that we have shaken off the dead weight of the past and created a genuinely twenty-first century institution, capable of adapting to and shaping a changing world. The benefit to students and teachers of experiencing this vigorous and dynamic environment will be enormous. We currently ask students to mold themselves to a static hierarchical school system and then go out into a dynamic networked world and perform competitively. This is an excellent example of how we need to rethink the overall relationship between schools and society. Society has moved on, but schools have moved very little.

This openness to the best ideas on learning and teaching, accompanied by a willingness to explore and pragmatically verify new practical approaches to every aspect of learning, will anchor the third component (the educational component), and ensure that we have three strong forces that stabilize and support the system against the powerful currents that inevitably accompany the birth of a new school system.

Those currents come from fundamental changes in our economy, our society and in our technology, which bring with them the opportunity for another huge leap in our health, wealth and culture, comparable to the consequences of the industrial revolution. Our economy is stimulating new ways of organizing our working life, which value workers for their individual intelligence and skills, and we are recognizing that the "mass" consumer culture is no longer the only way to have widespread access to goods and services. We are emerging as individuals from the anonymity of the group.

Technology is driving many of these changes and nowhere more so than in the production of knowledge.

Because the new technologies add wealth through information, they offer new ways to create, store and communicate knowledge, and history suggests that a new burst of knowledge and culture is starting to erupt. This new knowledge will be more inclusive and democratic in its creation and control, and will allow a much wider spectrum of "intelligences" to create and use it. School children especially will have fewer barriers to surmount, and will be able to learn more.

Finally we can create schools that nurture every child's intellectual curiosity, and support their motivation to learn and succeed. Every child can look forward to going to school to fulfill their own ambitions rather than competing against fellow students, and every parent can expect to find a sympathetic and professional response to their concerns.

So much of this is possible, and we cannot let the difficulties and dangers immobilize us. The time has come to shift our gaze from the problems of the old to the opportunities for a new school system, and start the conversation on how we can make the necessary changes.

QUESTIONS & ANSWERS

How can such a dramatic change be achieved?

We can envisage three broad scenarios. In the first we have an extended national conversation, driven by a recognition that we cannot reform the current system to meet future requirements, and followed by one or more States taking the lead to demonstrate the feasibility of the outcome of the national conversation. This is the scenario we discuss here. Secondly, we could "tinker" (to use Larry Cuban's phrase in "Tinkering Toward Utopia") towards a solution, driven by the logic of each required major change. This could achieve many of the goals set out here, but would lack the powerful emotional drive of a national commitment to a new approach. Thirdly we could emulate the nineteenth century Europeans and stick with our current ways until competitors force us to adapt, probably too late and with mixed results.

How do we start a national conversation?

The usual trigger for such a conversation is a crisis, but this seldom produces a thoughtful outcome. A better approach is to prepare for a crisis and use it when it happens to build support for the already prepared approach. Nor is a bottoms-up approach likely to succeed, because this naturally focuses on important near term problems at the expense of the structural changes. We are therefore suggesting a middle path of seeding a discussion among people who accept the need to make fundamental changes of the sort outlined in this book, and gradually draw into the conversation more and more stakeholders, who can provide the anchoring to reality that will eventually be necessary.

Is this a Federal initiative or one led by the States?

There is no bias in this proposal towards a Federal initiative, but it is intended to be adopted eventually by all the States. However, in a dynamic adaptive system, regional and local variations are to be expected and encouraged, provided the framework is recognized and adhered to. Inevitably the Social Compact will eventually require a nationwide consensus, but that too could emerge from an initiative by a few of the States. With respect to the curriculum, some parts (the New 3R's and a part of the New Civics Curriculum) are assumed to be determined by the States, but the majority of the curriculum and final certification is decided by Standards Boards' outside of the political or educational establishments.

How does this proposal compare to the existing reform efforts?

Reforms have been a constant feature of the public school landscape since its inception, with major bursts occurring after such crises as the launching of Sputnik in the 1950's. Today many efforts are attempting to leverage digital technologies to improve teaching and the organization of classrooms. A partial list of reform movements and experimental schools is given at the end of the Bibliography.

While many of them make a useful contribution to certain specific parts of the school system, so far all of them fail the key test - can they scale and transform the whole system. This failure is explained in the early part of this book as the consequence of three interlocking and deeply embedded design features that cause the current system to reject any changes incompatible with its industrial architecture or its interpretation of equal educational opportunity. As an analogy, attempts to seed entrepreneurial activities into a state controlled economy can have only limited success, because too much success would bring down the system. However, many of the current school reforms would flourish if embedded in an *fmf* school system, which is designed to encourage experimentation.

Doesn't this proposal favor the wealthier families?

Any large scale system with a set of rules or laws is subject to this challenge, and the best answer is to ensure that the gain for everyone is large in comparison to the differences in benefit. This was true when the current system replaced its predecessor, and the benefit overrode some obvious imperfections in the achievement of equal educational opportunity. Additionally, the *fmf* emphasis on personalized learning is a major improvement for many poorer families, since they have a higher likelihood of "special needs", as they are currently called. In the *fmf* system all students are special, and the political process can decide whether some students should receive extra funding. That said, many detailed design decisions can and should be adjusted to mitigate this concern.

Isn't this just another "progressive" proposal in disguise?

So many discussions about public schooling are framed in terms of labels that ensure that the reader or listener tunes out, and little progress is made. This work originated partly as a way to look at schools without those preconceptions, and to find basic ideas that could lead to a proposal with the minimum of such biases. The basic ideas are rooted in an attempt to understand fundamental changes in American society, and to design a public school system that is and will remain in harmony with society.

Personalization of learning is one of many personalizations changing key elements of society, such as healthcare, business, commerce and the armed service. The shift to dynamically linked networks of semi-independent functional units is occurring in those domains and many others. Similarly, the need to organize so that technology can transform work practices is a given in most fields, and becomes even more compelling when we grasp the fundamental changes in knowledge facing our students and teachers.

The main elements of the *fmf* school system were "discovered" by taking these trends seriously and assuming that they will dominate the lives of students in the coming decades. Once we see our task as preparing students for this radically different American society much of what appears in the proposal begins to seem obvious, even when reversing a century of practice.

Why does competition play such a small role in this proposal?

The proposed shift in attitude to competition between students can be understood by thinking about tennis and golf. To play a game of tennis <u>requires</u> that the players compete and try to defeat one another. Golf, on the other hand, is played against the course, and can additionally be turned into a competition between the players if they so agree. Our current view of schools resembles tennis and the *fmf* view resembles golf. The primary challenge for *fmf* students is to master the knowledge they require to achieve their future adult goals: some of them will be motivated by competing with other students, but many are far more motivated by their own possibilities and achievements. Competition has a role to play in preparing for life, but it is not central to acquiring knowledge, and it can be learned in many different ways by different students.

How will we know if an *fmf* school system is succeeding?

To misquote a Chinese saying, "Be careful what you test for!" Our understandable urge to measure school achievement and thereby reassure ourselves has played havoc with our schools and misdirected significant student and teacher energy, but we cannot simply hope for the best. The place to start is the recognition that, however we define success, it will ultimately depend on two very different contributors: the students and the schools. Punishing teachers for student failures makes as much sense as punishing parents for their children's misdemeanors. There is surely some blame, but there can be many causes.

The short *fmf* answer is to put the responsibility for student achievement squarely with the student/parent, and help them monitor success and take action when required. However, that leaves two questions: is society getting the results that it can reasonably expect from the system, and how well are individual schools performing. Society has two useful indicators of success: the feedback from the Standards Boards and an adapted form of the National Assessment of Educational Progress (NAEP), and other measures of societal goals could be formulated, such as the number of trained scientists.

The judgement of how well an individual school is performing comes partly from the student/parents, who vote with their feet by staying or going to another school, and partly by an annual audit overseen by the State Department of Education. While this audit does not directly assess educational performance, it does flag major indicators, such as changes in enrollment, changes in staffing and staff qualifications. We clearly need research to help characterize effective teaching.

Won't standards fall if students choose their curriculum?

Today we have a confusing idea of raising standards. A State Board responds to political pressure to raise standards and increases the content or difficulty of some part of the curriculum. Typically more children fail the test (or cheat), parents object and the standards are reset to the level at which political pressure dies down.

In going through this cycle we are misled by the literal interpretation of the word "standard." Simply raising the bar achieves no useful result if the teachers or students are incapable of increasing the performance of the students. There is an implicit assumption that either or both of the teachers or the students are underperforming relative to their capabilities, and that demanding more will achieve more. The little bit of truth in this assertion conceals the much larger flaw that we do not know how to improve student performance in the majority of schools, where so many factors affect the outcome for any given student or teacher.

Probably the single biggest contributor to student performance is student motivation, followed by teacher motivation and skill. We also know that motivation for any task tends to increase with the feeling of being in control, and with the strength of the emotional commitment to the goal. These are the drivers in the *fmf* school system: personal control and personal goals. It is also true that an outside stimulus, such as parental involvement, can make a huge difference, and *fmf* schools capitalize on this by requiring the student/parents to sign a contract with each school agreeing to the goals and responsibilities.

However, beyond the specific design features of the proposal there is an overarching recommendation that we change the national conversation about learning by shifting both the control and the responsibility to the student/parent (the Social Compact), and to proactively evangelize the value of learning and going to school. We have allowed the idea to become the norm, that parents drop their children at school and leave the rest to the teachers. While some parents are too stressed or too absent to play a useful role, building a support system around each student must be included in each school plan for the student, even if this detracts from some specific academic activity.

Doesn't the proposal ignore the social maturity of the student?

In the early years most students will be in a school with students of similar age, but, as each student progresses intellectually at their own pace, it is likely that different students of a given age will be studying at different intellectual levels. However, the intent is that much of the intellectual learning is done individually, not in large groups, and individual students participate in multiple groups during any one week. Schools will need to monitor and help students to manage their social interactions. Teachers will spend far less of their time teaching academic topics, and far more helping each student to become a mature manager of their own success.

APPENDIX 1.
TODAY'S CURRICULUM AND ITS CHALLENGES

PREDICTING THE FUTURE

What should students learn today to equip them for the world ten or twenty years in the future? Curriculum designers have always faced this question, but in recent years the rate of change in our society has made predicting the future very error prone. The natural response to this dilemma is to adapt the curriculum as needs change, but major curricular changes can wreak havoc in schools, and only modest regular changes can occur. As a result, the basic structure and much of the content must remain appropriate while society undergoes significant change. How can this be achieved?

Two basic strategies have evolved. The first aims to identify a specific list of basic knowledge skills and facts that will be valuable to virtually all adults as far into the future as we can hope to see. The key to success for this strategy is to keep the set of skills and facts to a very narrow range, selecting only those skills basic to many scenarios, because the more specialized the skill the more likely will change render it obsolete. For centuries, this strategy has given rise to the 3R's curriculum, with its emphasis on basic reading, writing and arithmetic. The choice has two practical advantages: most parents recognize what is being taught and understand why it is important, and there is a ready supply of capable teachers. Another variant of the same strategy is the Vocational curriculum, which attempts to prepare students for very specific jobs. It follows the long tradition of apprenticeships.

The second strategy takes almost the opposite approach, claiming that it is possible to avoid much of the problem by training students in intellectual skills of very general applicability, such as the ability to think clearly, to communicate and to analyze complex problems. This strategy generates our Liberal Arts curriculum, with its heritage stretching back to ancient Greece and Rome. It too has its variants, particularly the modern emphasis on critical thinking and 21st century skills.

Given their longevity and success, the two strategies must play a role in shaping the *fmf* Schools curriculum, but they both come with problems and baggage.

THE CURRENT 3R'S CURRICULUM

The main challenge to implementing a successful 3R's curriculum is easy to state but hard to address – every pressure on the curriculum is in one direction, expansion. The proponents of each addition can be passionate and compelling, but there are no offsetting advocates of removing topics or skills. At some point, curriculum growth reaches a self-defeating point, fostering a rag bag of special interests instead of a set of basic skills. Less academic students cannot afford this dissipation of their effort, and our advanced students lose the focus they need to learn an academically demanding curriculum.

The best hope of slowing down this inevitable growth is to erect a strong enough barrier, forcing additions to be traded for deletions. Prior to the development of the modern high school, there was such a natural barrier, because the 3R's curriculum was taught predominantly in Common Schools to students below the age of fourteen. Though not perfect, it constituted a stable outcome that was understandable by most parents, who subsequently supported the funding of public Common Schools teaching this curriculum.

This barrier was swept away with the introduction of the high school and the concept of the educational ladder, which required all students to be able to progress smoothly from a 3R's curriculum to a pre-college curriculum. For this reason, modern educators oppose the idea of a separate bounded 3R's curriculum, fearing that it leads to inappropriate streaming and steering of students into poor classes, based on conscious or unconscious bias. However this well intentioned ideal leads to very confusing conversations and dubious decisions about the curriculum, which now becomes one amorphous whole.

The issue of "higher standards" provides a classic example. Since most parents believe in higher standards - but few of them have any clear idea of how that translates into curricular decisions - they naturally default to a vague interpretation of an enhanced 3R's curriculum. Their logic makes perfect sense - there has been a sensible historical definition of basic educational skills, and it now needs to be updated to meet modern demands. But without a clear agreement of what we mean by basic, many elements of the current curriculum far exceed any commonly accepted meaning of basic, and the curriculum goes far beyond reading, writing and basic arithmetic. For example, today virtually all students learn how to find the Greatest Common Factor of two integers, but almost all promptly forget the procedure and seldom if ever use it in adult life. However, almost all adults benefit from fluency in using percentages, but many have a weak grasp of how to manipulate them, having been rushed past those lessons because the curriculum is so full. We have lost the ability to focus on the really basic parts of the curriculum and guarantee a minimum useful training for everyone.

This inflation of the basic curriculum was neatly captured in a Washington Post article (April 12th, 2004)

Virginia lists 41 "learning expectations" for fourth-grade math students in its statewide Standards of Learning. Maryland lists 67 in its Voluntary State Curriculum. The District has 45 standards.

If upgrading our standards adds even more "expectations", how are they going to fit into the fourth grade math text book which already has over 700 pages?

Inevitably major debates occur over what to keep and what to leave out, but the strict upper limit on the amount of material in the *fmf* Schools mandatory curriculum requires much of today's curriculum to be elective. As we shall argue shortly, this benefits students, teachers and society.

THE CURRENT VOCATIONAL CURRICULUM

We also need to understand some of the challenges associated with today's Vocational Curriculum. Like the 3R's curriculum, it results from focusing on some relatively simple intellectual skills, but uses a different criterion for choosing them. Instead of selecting for the widest applicability, the strategy selects for very specific future jobs, such as a motor mechanic. In one sense this simply denies the forecasting problem, by claiming that for certain jobs it is possible to predict the future and teach appropriate skills.

The strategy has appeared to work reasonably well for the last hundred years, while the US had an expanding industrial economy, but even so its fundamental premise has been questioned. Do students go into and stay in jobs for which they have been specifically trained, or have they simply used their more general 3R's skills to meet a high demand for general industrial workers? In other words, would the students and the country have achieved the same economic result without investing in vocational training in schools?

If the apparent past success of vocational schooling

is mostly attributable to having a stable expanding industrial economy, the same curricular strategy may be very unsuccessful in a more dynamic global economy, where millions of workers throughout the world have that same basic knowledge or better, and we no longer have the industrial supremacy to guarantee good salaries for people with modest knowledge skills. Long before we understand how much of the current curriculum was vital to our industrial success, the global marketplace will provide the answer, and it may come as an unpleasant surprise to many current students.

The problems associated with current vocational schooling extend to its implementation. The prevailing view is that less able teachers and students gravitate or are pushed towards this educational backwater and that many of the courses are ill-conceived, poorly equipped and not taken seriously by teachers or students. The worst are referred to as a "dumping ground". Good vocational courses exist, but for the time and money spent, vocational education must count as a failure. A significant contributing reason is its second class status.

Since schools today recognize only a certain type of academic achievement as the one real test of school success, vocational schooling must start with the stigma of being second rate. In a competitive system, only a few can really succeed, and everyone in the system knows it. As soon as students figure out where they stand in the academic race - or worse, as soon as teachers decide where they stand – some students are tracked into the "less able" classes. Only vocational students with a high degree of maturity and self-confidence see their path as leading to success. The others pass their time in the backwater, waiting until they can get out of school with its boring useless lessons. Lacking a strong positive identity, the vocational curriculum easily becomes another rag bag of pieces within the uniform curriculum.

The major force capable of counteracting this low status is missing from the current school system – the student has little or no say in what happens. The system figures out what is (supposedly) in the best interests of students and pushes them down that path. From this lack of power flow so many troubles: administrative convenience overwhelms student benefit, teachers' judgment replaces student motivation, school success with mainstream students takes precedence over maximizing the success of all students, and many more.

Unfortunately we have learned to accept these

results as inevitable. To be successful in implementing a vocational strategy, *fmf* schools need to raise its status, and give more control to the students who depend on it. Then students can develop pride in mastering the curriculum and teachers can proudly teach it.

THE CURRENT LIBERAL ARTS CURRICULUM

The 3R's curriculum and the Vocational curriculum both depend on selecting very specific and intellectually less demanding skills. By contrast, the Liberal Arts curriculum implements the complementary strategy of developing the student's broad intellectual skills.

In its purest form, the Liberal Arts curriculum goes beyond training students with intellectual skills, such as logical reasoning, by emphasizing wisdom, judgment, character and an awareness of the human condition seen through the eyes of great thinkers throughout the ages. This ideal curriculum has been the Holy Grail for educators for centuries. Today it appeals in several ways.

It removes the need to look forward and make messy judgments about the future; instead educators can look backwards at familiar territory. It has the practical advantage of leveraging the skills of academics trained in traditional disciplines, and having a ready-made and generally recognized structure of subjects and major topics. However this high degree of comfort is not shared by people who feel excluded from this traditional culture, and their demands lead to another watering down of the underlying strategy and another collection of rag bag items. One well documented example of watering down (See Ravitch, The Language Police) is the deterioration of text books, which more and more frequently replace examples of great classical writing by banal passages designed not to offend anyone.

Until recently the selection of the Liberal Arts curriculum has been a self-perpetuating scenario. Most people who think of themselves as educated use knowledge of its content as the benchmark, and with a good heart and clear conscience they can propose that all people will come to recognize its value, if only they are given the chance in school to appreciate it. Given the high esteem granted to this ideal curriculum, we have come to judge our schools by how many students master it. In truth very few do, but by watering it down sufficiently we can gain the appearance of success and thereby maintain the Holy Grail in place.

Setting college entrance as the most desirable outcome of schooling only reinforces the idea. Colleges keep intellectual life alive in a country more dedicated to material prosperity and personal satisfaction, and it is only natural that high schools, in seeing their most prestigious role as college preparation, should focus on the topics favored by academia.

In addition to these genuine advantages, some educators and commentators see the Liberal Arts curriculum as fulfilling another requirement - that it should provide us with a common core of knowledge that will bind us together and enhance our traditional values and way of life. They believe that all students should read similar books, know certain geographical and historical facts, and, in short, be educated to read a quality newspaper with good judgment and a prepared mind. Some point out that such an outcome would eliminate the Achievement Gap and go a long way towards our ideals of social justice.

The dream of a citizenry educated according the Liberal Arts curriculum has motivated thoughtful educators at least since Thomas Jefferson, who listed twenty-two desirable subjects for a pre-college school curriculum. Unfortunately the dream has never been realized for most Americans, as we can see by a quick glance at American life now or at any time in the last century. Despite giving generally high ratings to a curriculum of traditional subjects, such as history, geography and a foreign language, most parents do not intellectually engage with these subjects in their adult lives.

As a result of this disconnect, the "highbrow" culture implied by the Liberal Arts curriculum has only the remotest possibility of being a common unifying culture for the majority of Americans. American culture comes from the daily lives of ordinary citizens, and centers more on Seinfeld® and the results of the World Series than on Shakespeare or the Mona Lisa. In creating a working democracy we have allowed people to vote their cultural preferences with their feet, and they predominantly want TV series, sports, sound-byte news and human interest stories, rather than C-Span and lengthy political debates. They do not expect their Presidents to compare themselves to Caesar or quote Ovid (as Presidents might two hundred years ago).

This does not imply that Americans cannot think, or are unwilling to engage in meaningful debate on difficult subjects. Part of the peculiarly American political genius has been to allow the genuine tastes of the majority to triumph over those of the "educated" elite, without simultaneously preventing millions of people from enjoying the classical Western culture associated with the Liberal Arts curriculum. In contrast to many European countries, which still prefer visibly "educated" leaders, Americans prefer leaders who more visibly represent the tastes and manners of regular people, and in doing so make public what is true worldwide – high culture is a minority taste, not a candidate for uniting us.

Despite its intrinsic value and appeal to some parents, as a general solution to predicting the future, the true Liberal Arts curriculum has two fatal flaws: it plays little role in the daily life of the majority of American people and it cannot be made to work on a large scale. It is at best a partial solution to designing an effective modern curriculum.

Thus the three pillars of our current curricular strategy – the 3R's, Vocational education and the Liberal Arts curriculum – have too many flaws to generate directly the *fmf* Schools curriculum. However, when embedded in a system which corrects the problems visible in today's implementation, they take on a new lease of life and fulfill much of their original promise. This process is described in the Curriculum section of Chapter 4.

APPENDIX 2.
USEFUL DATA

ELEMENTARY AND SECONDARY EDUCATION

Enrollment

In fall 2018, about 56.6 million students will attend elementary and secondary schools, including 50.7 million students in public schools and 5.9 million in private schools. Of the public school students, 35.6 million will be in prekindergarten through grade 8 and 15.1 million will be in grades 9 through 12. The fall 2018 public school enrollment is expected to be slightly higher than the 50.6 million enrolled in fall 2017 and is higher than the 49.5 million students enrolled in fall 2010. Total public elementary and secondary enrollment is projected to increase between fall 2018 and fall 2027 to 52.1 million.

Of the projected 50.7 million public school students entering prekindergarten through grade 12 in fall 2018, White students will account for 24.1 million. The remaining 26.6 million will be composed of 7.8 million Black students, 14.0 million Hispanic students, 2.6 million Asian students, 0.2 million Pacific Islander students, 0.5 million American Indian/Alaska Native students, and 1.6 million students of Two or more races. The percentage of students enrolled in public schools who are White is projected to continue to decline through at least fall 2027 along with the percentage of students who are Black, while the percentage of students who are Hispanic Asian, and of Two or more races are projected to increase. (http://nces.ed.gov/programs/digest/d17/tables/dt17_203.60.asp)

In fall 2018, about 1.4 million children are expected to attend public prekindergarten and 3.6 million are expected to attend public kindergarten. (https://nces.ed.gov/programs/digest/d17/tables/dt17_203.10.asp)

About 4.0 million public school students are expected to enroll in 9th grade in fall 2018. Students typically enter American high schools in 9th grade.

Teachers

Public school systems will employ about 3.2 million full-time-equivalent (FTE) teachers in fall 2018, such that the number of pupils per FTE teacher—that is, the pupil/teacher ratio—will be 16.0. This ratio has remained consistent at around 16.0 since 2010. A projected 0.5 million FTE teachers will be working in private schools this fall, resulting in an estimated pupil/teacher ratio of 12.3, which is similar to the 2017 ratio of 12.2, but lower than the 2010 ratio of 13.0. (https://nces.ed.gov/programs/digest/d17/tables/dt17_208.20.asp)

Schools and Districts

In 2012–13, there were about 13,500 public school districts with nearly 98,500 public schools, including about 6,100 charter schools. In fall 2011, there were about 30,900 private schools offering kindergarten or higher grades.

Expenditures

Current expenditures for public elementary and secondary schools are projected to be $654 billion for the 2018–19 school year. The current expenditure per student is projected to be $12,910 for the 2018–19 school year. (https://nces.ed.gov/programs/digest/d17/tables/dt17_236.15.asp)

Attainment

About 3.6 million students are expected to graduate from high school in 2018–19, including 3.3 million students from public high schools and 0.4 million students from private high schools. (https://nces.ed.gov/programs/digest/d17/tables/dt17_318.40.asp)

Background information from prior school years:

Some information on the 2018–19 school year is not available. This section presents selected highlights from prior school years to provide some context for the current school year.

Elementary and Secondary Schools and Districts

In 2015–16, there were about 13,600 public school districts (source) with close to 98,300 public schools, including about 6,900 charter schools (source). In fall 2015, there were about 34,600 private schools offering kindergarten or higher grades (source).

In 2016–17, about one-third (32 percent) of districts reported that all of their Career and Technical Education (CTE) programs were structured as career pathways that align with related postsecondary programs, and an additional one-third (33 percent) reported that most of their programs were structured this way (source).

High School Dropout

The percentage of high school dropouts among 16- to 24-year-olds declined from 10.9 percent in 2000 to 6.1 percent in 2016 (source). Reflecting the overall decline in the dropout rate between 2000 and 2016, the rates also declined for White, Black, and Hispanic students.

This Appendix is a direct extract from the U.S. Department of Education, Institute of Education Sciences, 2018, National Center for Education Statistics.

A description of the National Assessment of Educational Progress (NAEP) can also be found at the National Center for Education Statistics

BIBLIOGRAPHY WITH COMMENTS

A personal selection of background reading on many different facets of US public schools. I have given ** to books that I think are particularly relevant to the development of the *fmf* proposal, and * to those that contribute to a good general understanding of particular issues or interesting proposals. This selection is not an endorsement or critique of any particular view of schooling, and is far from being complete in any sense.

*School:The Story of American Public Education.

James Anderson, Larry Cuban, Carl Kaestle, Diane Ravitch and David Tyack

Beacon Press (August 16, 2002)

> A companion volume to the PBS Series, "School", this is a very accessible account by established historians of the educational philosophies and debates that have shaped the public school system, while avoiding the harsher rhetoric that is present in some other accounts.

Reinventing the Bazaar: A Natural History of Markets.

John McMillan

W. W. Norton & Company; Reprint edition (November 17, 2003)

> A balanced view of how markets can succeed where central management cannot. It helps our understanding that markets are not always about monetary profit.

The Next Fifty Years: Science in the First Half of the Twenty-first Century.

John Brockman (editor)

Vintage; 1st edition (May 14, 2002)

> Twenty-five thinkers provide a wide ranging view of the possibilities facing students (and the rest of us) in the reasonably near future

The End of Education: Redefining the Value of School.

Neil Postman

Vintage; Reprint edition (October 29, 1996)

> A highly respected author proposes a different, more humanistic way to express the purpose of schools.

***Instead of Education: Ways to Help People do Things Better.**

John Holt

Sentient Publications; 2nd edition (October 1, 2003)

> John Holt wrote ten books on schooling, including the best seller How Children Fail (1964). This book "Instead of Education" is a critique of the standard approach to learning in schools and an implied encouragement towards home schooling. It connects to the *fmf* approach through its championship of changing the relationship of the student to the teacher and the school to the community.

Jefferson's Children: Education and The Promise of American Culture.

Leon Botstein

Doubleday; 1st edition (October 1997).

> Botstein, Dean of Bard College, argues for a more flexible school system, including having students leave school at age sixteen for a variety of educational or training facilities.

The Elements of Learning.

J.M. Banner Jr. and H.C. Cannon

Yale University Press. (September 1, 2001)

> Written as a guide to students, and filled with practical tips, it offers interesting insights into how students (can) learn in the expected environment of a classroom. It serves as a useful benchmark to assess whether any individual school or system of schools supports the process of learning or inhibits it.

The Schools our children deserve.
Alfie Kohn

Houghton Mifflin (1999)

> A leading critic of schools circa 1999, and a passionate advocate of the "constructivist" method, argue that it delivers as well on standardized tests, and has the added advantages that the learning lasts longer and the students enjoy it more.

Tinkering Toward Utopia: A Century of Public School Reform.
David Tyack and Larry Cuban

Harvard University Press, Cambridge Mass. 1995

> Two well respected authors offer a view opposite to the fundamental redesign approach of *fmf*, arguing that in the present system local teachers adapt proposed changes to be more realistic than any top-down approach can offer. He also discusses the Dalton Plan developed by Helen Pankhurst in the early 1920's, which emphasized the individual's freedom and responsibility, cooperation with other students and adults, and monthly contracts that teachers negotiated with students.

*The Quality School: Managing Students without Coercion
William Glasser M.D.

Harper Perennial; 3 Sub edition (July 9, 1998)

> Glasser applies W. E. Deming's ideas for quality management of industrial systems to schools, by treating students as the workers and teachers as the first line managers. He captures the point that the success of any organization depends on how well management manages. From the *fmf* perspective, this book stays too close to the industrial management approach, and loses the full potential value of applying Deming's ideas to schools.

*The Power of Their Ideas.

Deborah Meier.

Beacon Press (August 16, 2002)

> Deborah Meier made a powerful impact on educators by her reforms within the New York City School System and later in Boston, and this captures her ideas and convictions about how schools should work. She proposes that a school should be not only child-centered but community-centered as well, integrating possibly several schools into a community centered unit. The book is valuable for the practical hands-on experience that Meier brings to the discussion.

**The Horace Books.

Theodore H. Sizer

Horace's Compromise: The Dilemma of the American High School. (1984)

Horace's School: Redesigning the American High School: Houghton Mifflin (1984)

Horace's Hope. Mariner Books (1997)

> The trilogy, together with Sizer's other books, offer a significant contribution to the ideas and practice of school reform. Sizer lays out a coherent set of ideas for how schools could best function within the confines of the existing framework, with a strong focus on the involvement of parents and the local community.
>
> Horace's Compromise is the first book, and, by following the life of a fictional teacher (Horace), identifies the problems in schools, especially those facing teachers.
>
> Horace's School is an attempt to show how a school might go about changing itself along the lines of an "Essential School".
>
> Horace's Hope lays out specific plans for a community based school., including staffing ratios, timetables and many details that are important to achieving his vision of a high school.
>
> His views would flourish within the *fmf* system.

**Smart Schools: Better thinking and learning for every child.

David Perkins.

The Free Press. 1992

> A very relevant and thoughtful contribution to understanding how students learn. His educational goals include retention of knowledge, understanding of knowledge, and active use of knowledge, and he emphasizes important *fmf* topics, such as motivation, and authentic assessment.

*The Disciplined Mind.

Howard Gardner

Penguin Books; 1st edition (2000)

> A thoughtful discussion, as seen by a cognitive scientist, of how schools arrived at their then current (2000) state, and how to move forward. The book is especially interesting to the *fmf* approach for its focus on individuality and motivation, and its emphasis on the value of studying the thought processes required in different disciplines.

A Legacy of Learning: Your Stake in Standards and New Kinds of Public Schools.

David T Kearns and James Harvey.

Brookings Institution Press; First Edition edition (March 1, 2000)

> David Kearns, the Chairman Emeritus of New American Schools and the former Chairman of the Xerox Company gives this book the flavor expected of an executive who sees a failing system and knows how to fix it. However, some of the prescriptions fit well with the *fmf* approach, especially those that emphasize parental choice (though not student choice) and schools operating independently of the state under a contract. Unfortunately it seems to veer to the Charter School version of reform within the current constraints, which does not work well and does arouse much antagonism. The *fmf* approach attempts to use some of the same ideas in a framework that improves the standing of teachers and students, and does not feel like reform from above.

A Nation at Risk: The Imperative for Educational Reform.

National Commission on Excellence in Education

University of Michigan Library (January 1, 1983)

> The report "to the nation and the Secretary of Education" that started many efforts at reform, and included the memorable lines: "*If an unfriendly foreign power had attempted to impose on America the mediocre educational performance that exists today, we might well have viewed it as an act of war. As it stands, we have allowed this to happen to ourselves.*" Many opponents saw it as a propaganda piece that found the facts to support a predetermined conclusion, but it has had undeniable impact.

American Schools, Blueprints for School Success:

A Guide to New American Schools Designs

Educational Research Service, Arlington, Va.: (1998).

> An example of a specific alternative "blueprint" that has achieved a level of acceptance, but lacks the radical changes deemed necessary in the *fmf* system.

*Predicting the Behavior of the Educational System.

T F Green

Syracuse Univ Pr (Sd); 1st edition (June 1980)

> An unusual view of schools focusing on the system aspects. Though not written for a general audience it offers a clear exposition of the system elements that lead to specific characteristics of our current system, and is refreshingly devoid of the emotional debates that afflict most discussions on schools.

*One Kid at Time: Big Lessons from a Small School.

Eliot Levine

Teachers College Press (November 1, 2001)

> A fascinating account of a particular school, the Met School in Rhode Island, which would fit well within the *fmf* school system. It discusses many of the educational ideas presented in our Chapter 4, with the benefit of real experience to illustrate the points.

Redesigning Public Education: the Kentucky Experience.

J. D. Foster

Diversified Services Inc. (September 15, 1999)

> A thoughtful concrete proposal for school reform created by a Kentucky State Task Force and implemented in more than 50 schools.

*How's my Kid doing? A Parent's Guide to Grades, Marks, and Report Cards.

Thomas R. Gusskey

Jossey-Bass; 1st edition (March 14, 2003)

> He discusses the methods of assessment and their pluses and minuses. A useful primer on testing, as background to any proposal for reform.

1600 Perfect Score: the Seven Secrets of Acing the SAT.

Tom Fischgrund

HarperCollins Publishers; (October 13, 2009)

> An account of the lifestyles and study habits of SAT perfect-score achievers, in the era when the SAT perfect score was 1600. An interesting antidote to the many books that concentrate on failing students.

Brief Intervals of Horrible Sanity.

Elizabeth Gold

Tarcher (October 7, 2004)

> As the blurb says, "an acerbic, humorous account of one poet-cum-teacher's experience at a "New Visions" high school in Queens, New York." A rather dark view of school life, especially of a new "alternative" school.

*Children as Pawns:The Politics of Educational Reform.

Timothy A. Hacsi

Harvard University Press (September 1, 2003)

> A rare examination of how practice compares to the

known research on five major reform topics: Head Start; Bilingual education; Small class size; Social promotion; School funding;

Education and Capitalism: Struggles for Learning and Liberation.
Sarah Knopp, Jeff Bale

Haymarket Books (April 17, 2012)

> An example of the emotional commitment to one of two dominant views of what is wrong with our public schools, written by self-described teacher-activists.

*There are no Shortcuts.
Rafe Esquith

Anchor; Reprint edition (May 11, 2004)

> A multi-award winning teacher at a Los Angeles Elementary School gives a personal account that captures the unending commitment and time demanded by the unrealistic goals that he somehow manages to achieve. At once heart-warming and frightening to all would-be reformers.

Fires in the Bathroom: Advice for Teachers from High School Students.
Kathleen Cushman

The New Press (April 1, 2005)

> A chance to hear the voices of high school students, through extensive interviews at schools in several urban areas.

*The Right to Learn: A Blueprint for Creating Schools that Work.
Linda Darling-Hammond

Jossey-Bass; first edition (August 3, 2001)

> A highly respected academic committed to the classic idea of a liberal education offers a learner-centered vision of that ideal.

Testing for Learning.

Ruth Mitchell

Free Press (September 12, 2007)

> One person's alternative to multiple choice testing.

The Flickering Mind: Saving Education from the False Promise of Technology.

Todd Oppenheimer

Random House (December 18, 2007)

> An account of how the blind application of computers in the classroom can not only fail, but backfire. Its description of technology in the classroom should not be confused with the proposals in this book!

Primal Teen: What New Discoveries about the Teenage Brain Tell about Our Kids

Barbara Strauch

Anchor; Reprint edition (September 14, 2004)

> The author, medical science and health editor at the New York Times, offers insights into adolescent behavior based on research and interviews with adolescents.

*The Educational Writings of John Locke.

James L. Axtell

Cambridge University Press 1968

> For those brave enough to go back and read the original ideas of a great thinker.

Some Thoughts Concerning Education.

John Locke

Original Edition, London 1705

Recent Publication by NuVision Publications, 2007.

> A reminder that we did not always relate to children how we do today.

*In Schools We Trust. Creating Communities of Learning in an Era of Testing and Standardization

Deborah Meier

Beacon Press 2002

> Based on the success of small public schools she and her colleagues created in Boston and New York. she advocates trusting teachers and students and parents to use their own judgment - an approach that would work well within the *fmf* school system.

*The Paideia Proposal.

Mortimer J. Adler

Touchstone (October 1, 1998)

> Amongst other positions, Adler was Director of the Institute for Philosophical Research, and this book, published under their auspices on behalf of The Paideia Group, is perhaps the best example of an approach to reform by returning to the true ideals of the classical Liberal Arts tradition.

**American Education. The National Experience 1783-1876

Lawrence J Cremin

Harpercollins; 1st edition (August 1980)

> The second of Cremin's outstanding trilogy, (see also The Colonial Experience and the Metropolitan Experience.) The structuring of the *fmf* proposal around the three fundamental forces owes much to the insights in this history.

*Making Good Citizens. Education and Civil Society.

Diane Ravitch & Joseph P. Viteritti

Yale University Press (August 1, 2003)

> A series of essays by a range of authors exploring the connection between education and citizenship, and a vital contribution to the belief that *fmf* schools must have a very strong commitment to a New Civics Curriculum.

**Left Back: A Century of Battles over School

Reform.

Diane Ravitch

Simon & Schuster (August 7, 2001)

> A leading educational historian offers a balanced perspective on the conflicting views that have shaped the school system.

The Language Police: How Pressure Groups Restrict What Students Learn.

Diane Ravitch

Vintage; Reprint edition (May 11, 2004)

> Here Ravitch offers an inside look at how political pressures affect the curriculum and the text books.

The Bell Curve: Intelligence and Class Structure in American Life.

Richard J. Herrnstein and Charles Murray

Free Press; 1st Free Press (January 10, 1996)

> A provocative and highly disputed account of the disparate origins and endowments of intelligence in people, and an interpretation of their impact on society. Worth reading, if only to understand a significant opinion to disagree with!

So Much Reform, So Little Change: The Persistence of Failure in Urban Schools.

Charles M. Payne

Harvard Education Press (April 30, 2008)

> An updated version of the difficulties of reforming the current system.

**How People Learn: Brain, Mind, Experience, and School

The National Academies Press, Washington D.C., (1999)

*How Students Learn: History, Mathematics and Science in the Classroom",

The National Academies Press, Washington D.C., (2005)

AN ALTERNATIVE VIEW

To provide one alternative view of the topics that are important for education reform, here is a list compiled by Amanda Kay Oaks (February, 2017) of "8 books to read if you want to make American education great again" posted on the BOOKRIOT website.

1. *American Education: A History* by Wayne J. Urban and Jennings L. Wagoner, Jr.
2. *Savage Inequalities* by Jonathan Kozol
3. *What Does it Mean to be Well Educated?* by Alfie Kohn
4. *Waiting for "Superman": How We Can Save America's Failing Public Schools* by Karl Weber
5. *The Life and Death of the American School System: How Testing and Choice are Undermining Education* by Diane Ravitch
6. *Teaching Community: A Pedagogy of Hope* by bell books
7. *The Smartest Kids in the World: And How They Got That Way* by Amanda Ripley
8. *Other People's Children: Cultural Conflict in the Classroom* by Lisa Delpit

ORGANIZATIONS AND SCHOOLS ACTIVE IN THE REFORM MOVEMENT (2018)

The numbering and diversity of groups attempting to change or experiment with new types of schools, ways of teaching and curricula is extraordinary. Although none of them show signs of becoming a dominant model for most schools, they do illustrate the new possibilities that will become available, when we find the right system to support and encourage them.

The following lists are intended to illustrate that diversity, but not to endorse any of them specifically. The lists are far from a complete.

A listing of National Reform School Initiatives can be found at the University of Illinois at Urbana-Champaign: http://www.library.illinois.edu/sshel/education/ilschoolreform/nationalinitiatives.html

Education Resources Information Center (ERIC) has a Catalog of School Reform Models. (http://eric.ed.gov/?id=ED458703)

A collection of recent programs:
- Accelerated Schools
- ACHIEVE
- America's Choice Design Network
- ATLAS Communities
- Big Picture Learning
- Business Roundtable
- Center on the Developing Child
- Coalition of Essential Schools (see Sizer)
- CO-NECT Schools
- Core Knowledge Foundation
- Council for Basic Education
- The Education Trust
- Expeditionary Learning
- Modern Red Schoolhouse
- National Board for Professional Teaching Standards
- The National School Reform Faculty
- New American Schools
- Purpose-Centered Education
- Roots and Wings
- School Reform Initiative (SRI)
- School Development Program
- Success for All
- Urban Learning Centers

41 Innovative K-12 Schools chosen by NOODLE (www.noodle.com)

Public
- Clairemont Elementary School
- Clintondale High School
- Ewa Makai Middle School
- Francis C. Hammond Middle School
- Grand Rapids Public Museum School
- Harvey Milk High School
- Lake View High School

Loving High School

MAST Academy

Pathways in Technology Early College High School

Quest to Learn

Vail Ski & Snowboard Academy

Vergennes Union High School

Visitacion Valley Middle School

Wyoming Indian Elementary School

The Young Women's Leadership School of East Harlem

Zoo School

Private

AltSchool

Avenues: The World School

The Center School

Crossroads School for Arts & Sciences

DePaul Cristo Rey High School

Fusion Academy

Interlochen Arts Academy

The Mountain School

Saint Ann's School

Shady Hill School

Sudbury Valley School

THINK Global School

Charter

Alliance School

Compass Charter School

Democracy Prep Public Schools

e3 Civic High

Evergreen Community Charter School

FirstLine Schools

Harlem Children's Zone Promise Academy

Charter Schools

KIPP Public Charter Schools

Minnesota New Country School

Richard Wright Public Charter School for Journalism and Media

STAR School

Uncommon Schools

www.ingramcontent.com/pod-product-compliance
Lightning Source LLC
Chambersburg PA
CBHW052145110526
44591CB00012B/1860